Leaving No Child Behind:
50 Ways to Close the Achievement Gap

Leaving No Child Behind:
50 Ways to Close the Achievement Gap

Standards for High Performing Schools Series

Lead Author and Editor
Carolyn J. Downey

Contributing Authors:
Larry E. Frase
William K. Poston, Jr.
Betty E. Steffy
Fenwick W. English
R. Gerald Melton

Curriculum Management Systems, Inc.

Statement of Intellectual Property Rights

Curriculum Management Systems, Incorporated (CMSi) and its licensors retain all ownership rights to this intellectual property and printed matter, including any or all related documentation. Use of this published material is governed by law, and all rights for copying or reproducing this published material in any manner are reserved exclusively to CMSi.

Copyright law prohibits copying or reproducing this published material without explicit written permission from CMSi. Making unauthorized copies, adaptations, presentations, or characteristics is prohibited and constitutes a punishable violation of the law. CMSi may revise this published material from time to time without notice.

This published material is provided "as is" without warranty of any kind. In no event shall CMSi be liable for any direct, indirect, special, exemplary, incidental, or consequential damages of any kind arising from any error in this published material or from any use or application of it, intended or unintended, including and without limitation any loss or interruption of business or revenue, however caused, and on any theory of liability, whether in contract, strict liability, or tort (including negligence or otherwise).

The views and opinions expressed in this published material are those of the authors and do not necessarily represent the views of CMSi.

Published by:

Curriculum Management Systems, Inc.
6165 NW 86th Street
PO Box 857
Johnston, IA 50131
Phone: (515) 727-1744 Fax: (515) 727-1743
Email: cmsi@curriculumsystems.com   Website: www.curriculumsystems.com

Publication Coordinator: William K. Poston Jr.
Production Assistance: K. Schweer, H. J. Kaptain, K. Flug
Editing Assistance: H. M. Boeschen, Lynn Meinecke
Cover Design: Greg Morrill
Photos and Graphics: Getty Images, Inc., Christian Hansen
Publishing Consultant: Robert Peitzman
Printed in the U.S.A. by Acme Printing, Des Moines, IA 50314

TABLE OF CONTENTS

Foreword

About CMSi

Curriculum Management Systems, Inc., is a corporation dedicated to the improvement and enhancement of educational performance and results through curriculum and assessment design and delivery, optimization of system activities and resources, and the ethic of working smarter instead of harder for change. The company was founded in 1996 under the name of Curriculum Management Audit Centers, Inc., but demands for its services and products have grown exponentially into programs and services for professional educators, school systems, and policy making bodies.

CMSi is still developing and evolving and its primary objective is to continue to provide support for the expansion and improvement of governance, leadership, direction, congruity, feedback, and productivity of educational institutions.

About This Book

This book represents a labor of love by six distinguished educational leaders who collectively represent over 225 years of professional experience in public education. The book is a capstone effort by these six individuals and is aimed at exemplifying the best practice and knowledge gleaned from the background, training, and experience of the past four decades.

This book provides important research and practical information on how to cope with high-stakes tests in the decidedly politicized environment currently facing school administrators, teachers, parents, and patrons. Never before in our history has so much weight been placed on the tested performance of students on mandated state tests. Given this highly challenging environment, the authors compiled what they have learned over several decades that will positively impact the level and extent of student test performance and measured achievement. Educational leaders and practitioners are the intended recipients of these precepts as they move to raise the achievement levels of *all* students.

Any tool worth its salt must work well in the situation for which it was designed. This book is designed to be a tool for school leaders and others to conduct a self-diagnosis of their educational system for the purpose of maximizing student achievement. Underscoring the need for this tool is the fact that students have different, contrasting needs, which diminishes the likelihood that any single approach, strategy, or program will suit the needs of a broad spectrum of students. Given that fact, this book is structured to provide a wide variety of approaches and strategies suitable for a wide spectrum of students. In essence, this book follows a plan in full acknowledgement that "one size does not fit all."

We commit this work of love to all those who labor every day to make learning come alive for all students from all backgrounds and with all diversity in the classroom.

Preface

Creating High Performing Schools: It Isn't Just about the Curriculum!

There is no mystery to developing high-performing schools. The major problem is how educators, schooling critics, and many within the public think about them. Typically, low-performing schools conjure up images of poor teaching, lazy or unmotivated faculty, incompetent administrators, overcrowded classrooms, outdated textbooks, or tragically stupid, hostile, or unmotivated students. A low-performing school is considered "bad," and the traditional remedies run the gamut from doing more work ("better" planning, staff development, class-size reduction, technology, curriculum change, some off-the-shelf new, remedy) to doing something different (extending the school day, parent tutors, community involvement, uniforms, block scheduling, peer collaboration) to doing away with them (academic bankruptcy, probation, intervention, takeover, privatization, vouchers, etc.)

None of these approaches address the true nature of the problem. Rather than jumping to a solution designed to solve the problem of low student performance, (low-performing schools), the strategies recommended in these pages begin at the end and work back. The end is how low-performing schools are identified through an evaluation instrument of some sort-usually by one or more tests. Thus, the solution to the problem begins by separating out the evaluation instrument and trying to determine:

- How the instruments in use define learning and teaching, both implicitly and explicitly;
- How the assessment selects exactly which learnings will be measured;
- How measured learnings and sub-learnings can be tracked back to specific materials provided to teachers to teach, (normally called a curriculum);
- Which learnings and sub-learnings that are included in the curriculum are also included on the test, and which of those learnings are not on the test;
- Which learnings and sub-learnings not included in the curriculum are on the test, at least to the point of test mastery (developing a supplementary curriculum).

In short, *it is the test or assessment instrument that defines what performances are to be expected.* It is the testing norms that define acceptable levels of performance. These are not established by the curriculum. Curriculum standards are independent of test specifications. In many cases, the curriculum framework is so nebulous that a test actually represents a further delineation of the curriculum rather than a congruent measurement of it. That is why working from an inadequate curriculum framework will not improve test scores unless one is unusually lucky.

The educator who understands the problem must begin by understanding that a low-performing school has been identified by a test of student learning, and that assessment is but a sample of all the learning going on in any school. Understanding the nature of sampling, knowing what and where school learning will be sampled, and ensuring that tested learning will be adequately taught to students represents the means to remove a school from the category of low-performing, and that's all it means. It doesn't necessarily mean that the school suddenly becomes "good." All it means is that the performance that the test is sampling looks better within the boundaries of the test. There are a lot of good schools whose test scores are low.

In short, performance is always defined by the instrument measuring and defining it, not by the curriculum that included it nor the teacher who taught it. The test is the final arbiter of performance. And we all know that tests aren't perfect. That is why it is even more critical to know something about the dynamics of raising student test scores by starting with the test instead of ending with its administration.

The bottom line is pretty simple: *Don't surprise the kids!* Tests that surprise children translate into a measurement for that which they were not taught and didn't learn. A second corollary is *don't surprise the teachers!* Chances are that if teachers are surprised, students will also be surprised. We advocate in this publication the doctrine of *no surprise for teachers and children.*

Tests of accountability are not primarily diagnostic. They are designed to or result in the establishment of a foundation for legal and often punitive actions on the part of state agencies and authorities against administrators, teachers, students and certain school communities. These communities are often those most in need of help-children of the poor and of color. The well-documented correlation between SES, gender, and race runs through the testing literature for at least three decades, and that's no accident. Avoiding serious interrogation of the tests at the end of the sequence simply perpetuates the status quo. In fact, for schools serving the poor, there is no way off the bottom of an imposed bell curve without paying strict attention to the parameters, content, and testing protocols embodied on the instrument that identifies low-performing schools.

This book is about how to unmask the variables and practices that account for low-performing schools and turn them into high-performing schools.* It's about how to put an end to the self-fulfilling and false prophecies that poverty or certain gender and race automatically translate into low test performance. It is about opportunity. It is about equity. It is about fairness. It begins with knowing where to start. Whatever defines performance and the norms regarding low, middle, and high-performance, *it isn't just the curriculum!*

---

* For more information about conducting an external evaluation review based on the principles outlined in this book, contact: Curriculum Management Systems, Incorporated (CMSi)
        Dr. William K. Poston, Jr., Executive Vice President
        Main Office: 6165 NW 86th Street, P. O. Box 857 Johnston, IA 50131
        Phone: (515) 727-1744 Fax: (515) 727-1743
        Email: cmsi@curriculumsystems.com

Introduction

Getting It Together: The Heart of the Matter

The heart of the matter is all about connecting the internal operations (various forms of teaching) to the curriculum that has been aligned (made congruent) with the battery of tests used to assess student performance, and doing so in a way that produces consistent test score gains over time, even if the test is changed at any specific point in time. Clearly this requires an in-depth understanding of the forces at work in the school-curriculum-teaching-testing relationship.

This linkage between the taught, written and tested curricula has been called "quality control" when viewed from the perspective of developing institutional (human) capacity. Quality control refers to the capability of any given educational unit (district, school, classroom, group) to link these three elements together so that are well aware of what is going to be tested (or evaluated), irrespective of the form of that evaluation.

For accountability to become a fair practice in schools, each aspect of quality control must be present at each unit or subunit to be assessed. And it is clear that some of the elements comprising quality control are beyond the purview of any individual classroom teacher or principal. Some of the critical components are the responsibilities of the school system and/or the state educational apparatus.

While the idea of connecting the three elements (taught, written, and tested curricula) at each level has long been recognized as the essence of sound curricular practice, today we know we also need to focus on the direction and intensity of these connections. Connecting testing and teaching is generally understood to produce better testing results, and few teachers object to teaching their own test and consider it good practice to do so-the *what to be learned* is the same as the *what to be tested*. However, when the *what to be learned* is not the same as the *what to be tested* (as in the case of a state mandated test) the issue of the dominance of the test is raised. In this circumstance many teachers feel the test is an unwarranted intrusion and resent its unhelpful interference in their decisions about what to teach on a daily basis. When it is the agency of the state that has selected the test, and the test is obviously not a measure of any specific local curriculum, nor of a state curriculum, the propriety of the test is brought fully into question. When such tests are elevated to tests of accountability and are used to reward or punish teachers, schools, and/or school districts, teaching practices such as alignment fall into gray areas.

About thirty-seven years of research show rather clearly that student performance on unaligned tests correlate strongly with socio-economic, demographic variables of students and their families, and school-controlled variables are either not significant or have little influence on how well students do on them. One result is that when low scoring schools are required to engage in additional planning and work because of student responses on tests that are unaligned or poorly aligned to a local curriculum, no school activity will improve scores appreciably until what is tested is taught.

The Local school systems must shift their teaching to what is tested because that is the only way the test can become a fair and/or reliable measure of what is taught, thus negating whatever diagnostic capacity the test contained. If they ignore the test and engage in activities that, while interesting, will not significantly improve student performance on the test, no significant and consistent gains will be made over time.

The testing gurus who advise us on what constitutes so-called ethical or appropriate behavior, but who have little control over the inappropriate legislation that drives such practices, are often not very helpful because their "ethics" involve all parties who have decision-making authority in the teaching/testing equation. In fact the catch-22 in which local educators often find themselves when the norm-referenced tests are mandated as the state's official exam, is that they either work from tests *back* to curriculum or they ignore the tests. In the first instance they may be accused of engaging in unethical or inappropriate responses, or suffer the consequences of having educational responsibilities for educating the children of the poor who are most often ethnic minorities.

On the other hand, simply teaching to the publicly released test content, even while acceptable under most conditions, may indeed produce a one-time bump in test scores but fail to produce the long-term, consistent gains which are the hallmark of a successful school-based intervention. Teaching to the test on the basis of publicly released items is the place to start the process of alignment, but without moving to deep alignment practices that go beyond teaching only test content on any specific form of a test, the prospect of attaining consistent test score gains over time is doubtful.

Connecting the three elements (written, taught, and tested curricula) at each level, particularly in the classroom, raises many significant and controversial issues. Among them are:

- Teaching to the test and ethical behavior as it pertains to the relationship between assessment and instruction;
- The efficacy of state educational mandates and state mechanisms of control and enforcement/inspection as it involves high-stakes testing and the impact of these trends on local educational practices;
- The autonomy and professionalism of the classroom teacher functioning within a state-directed and controlled educational system;
- The relationship between schools and the state as it manifests itself in translating societal expectations about schools and student behavior.

We will address these issues in this publication. For those schools serving large numbers of children of the poor, creating a fair system in which the actual talents and learning of all children are assessed means creating practices that sustain consistent test score gains. This book offers fifty strategies that when implemented will not only create schools where all children learn, but will also create schools capable of achieving at high-performance levels as defined by the tests in use.

❧ Six Standards for High Performing Schools

Creating and Implementing Constancy of Purpose

Perhaps the best overall guide for discussing the six standards for high-performing schools is W. Edward Deming's concept of *constancy of purpose (1986)*[1]. These three words embody the essence of how to create a high-performing school.

Implicit in Deming's idea is that a successful organization requires a purpose, that is, a clear sense of direction, a unified and strategic focus. In schools, this purpose must relate to goals and objectives regarding student learning. Such objectives must be valid, clear, and compelling. They must embody significant national and international standards. They must be understood by everyone involved in teaching children and by those monitoring the delivery of the instructional program. In curriculum auditing, the notion of purpose is embedded in the idea of *curriculum design (English/Poston, 1999)*[2].

The second part of quality is contained in the word *constancy*. Constancy means staying power under duress. It pertains to consistency in orientation when examining related problems in schools even if that institutional capacity has undergone change. Implicit in the idea of institutional capacity building is installing quality control as a part of the infrastructure in which the written, taught, and tested curricula are connected, integrated, and interactive. It means when one of these three elements changes or is changed, the others will and should also change. Constancy involves undergirding the day-to-day operations of schools in teaching, administering, assessment, motivating, linking, modifying and working for improved gains. While it is largely concerned with curriculum delivery, constancy, this "hanging in there" attitude, is established through curriculum design.

Let's examine these six critical standards for high-performing schools one by one.

STANDARD ONE: Establish a Well-Crafted, Focused, Valid, and Clear Curriculum to Direct Teaching

Curriculum is the fundamental work plan for what goes on in schools. It not only embodies organizational philosophy, but it also incorporates the legal and operational requirements within which schools function. In the past, curriculum has meant just about anything that could be conceived within schools. It represented not only aspirations and

---

[1] Deming, W.E. (1986). *Out of the Crisis.* Cambridge, MA: MIT Press.
[2] English, F. W., & Poston, W. K., Jr. (eds). (1999). *GAAP: Generally Accepted Audit Principles for Curriculum Management.* Johnston, Iowa: CMSi Press.

lofty social goals, but it also embodied challenging the social order with objectives that were radically opposed to the existing class structure.

While curriculum may be regarded as incorporating revolutionary content and the intellectual agenda of either the political left or right, in the model of high-performing schools it is primarily focused on attaining the goals and objectives explicit and implicit in the program of testing and assessment. This is not a politically naive decision on the part of curriculum workers. Rather, if schools do not demonstrate their capacity to attain even a modest range of general mainstream purposes, the trend is already unmistakably clear. Such low-performing schools are dealt with harshly and punitively, perhaps even put out of business by a kind of fiduciary slow death, or even abolished in the name of academic bankruptcy.

In addition to valid and clear curriculum content, the curriculum of the high-performing school has to be modest and not grandiose. Achieving constancy of purpose requires that teachers and administrators have a reasonable number of goals and objectives to attain. Such goals and objectives should be capable of being achieved and not overwhelming. The easiest way to accomplish this is to limit the goals and objectives to be pursued, at least initially, to those tested.

This tenet usually brings howls and protests not only from teachers who fear a loss of control over curriculum content, but also from curriculum developers who understand that tests are just samples of the whole curriculum, as well as from assessment directors who also understand the limitations of the types of learning their tests embody. We find these arguments ill-conceived, even illogical. If it is performance as defined by any test that results in the imposition of sanctions or rewards, then the content embodied in the measuring tool should trigger those same positive and/or negative responses. Informing teachers and administrators that they should not be too concerned, or that they should dump other things in the curriculum to spend time solely or exclusively on the tested curriculum is to confess that:

- The test is not all that important and may not be assessing the most important learning that could be taught (why then is it attached to rewards and/or sanctions?); and/or
- The attainment of high-performance by any group on any test requires a concentration of resources and less attention to that which will not result in success. Failing to emphasize actions that lead to a concentration of resources on priority targets undermines organizational effectiveness and detracts from the capacity of the school to improve student achievement.

Finally we note that the current popular notion of assessment driven instruction is a clear message that teaching should be and must be connected to tests in use. Reformers see tests being used as the device to ratchet up learning.

It should be clear that at least for curriculum development the concept of high performance is reductionistic; that is, since performance is defined and bordered, it both promotes concentration of resources and discourages resources from being expended on content not included within the boundaries of performance. Teachers and administrators who fail to grasp the clear implication of becoming a high-performance school usually do not understand the meaning of *constancy*. Not everything has the same priority in a high-performance school. Some things are much more important than others. The final arbiter of the matter of importance is the tested curriculum.

Another aspect of constancy within this standard is that curriculum should be easy to use, or "user- friendly." High-performing schools have teachers and administrators who are not afraid to try different formats for curriculum materials. They understand that connecting the written, taught, and tested curricula can take a variety of forms as long as the essential connectivity and clarity are not compromised. They are also not fooled into thinking that superficial uniformity or standardization is not an important matter and will not promote constancy if it is not functional. There are differences in the ways various curricular content are conceptualized and set into a work plan. Essential skills tend to require a different shaping than essential content. There will be differences between elementary and secondary curriculum guides.

STANDARD TWO: Provide Assessments Aligned to the Curriculum

Curriculum provides focus and connectivity from the work of classroom teachers and how that effort fits into an overall structure of defined performance. All of this can take place in the absence of specific assessment strategies or tools. But with the advent of high-stakes testing that essentially defines the nature of performance itself, curriculum development must include alignment to the tests in use. This ensures that the energy of teachers and administrators will result in improved student performance on the instrument that has defined the nature of improvement and that will also become the triggering device for rewards and sanctions.

Alignment not only means matching tested content to curriculum content, it also means engaging in *deep parallelism* that ensures congruence between the tested and written curriculum. We have learned that since alignment has become popularized, nearly every school or district claims that it is aligned. A close inspection, however, demonstrates that the matching that has occurred is often superficial. "Drill and kill" worksheets have proliferated in schools located in states where high-stakes tests are in use. Such responses will not result in sustained student gains and will also produce classrooms of incredible boredom and mindlessness. Learning in such places has been tragically dumbed down.

Responses to high-stakes testing in the superficial vein amounts to lobotomizing teachers and students. Schools and the curriculum have been debased.

Engaging in deep alignment results in instruction that extends far beyond the test. It means that teachers anticipate the directions in which the test may be moving. It means that teachers focus on the underlying principles and processes involved in truly comprehending and mastering the multiple learnings that are a part of every single test item included on any given test. In short, the practice of deep alignment is *teaching to the test that is not yet created*, and while it begins with current assessment, it runs far more broadly and deeply than with just the tests in use. It is necessary to understand current test logic, protocols, norms, objectives, format, item construction, content domain sampling, weighting and frequency of questions within the test, and overall content coverage, but even this is clearly not enough. This is where high-performing schools start but it is not where they end. High-performing schools are in an *anticipatory mode* as it pertains to any test in use. Non-high-performing schools are in a *reactionary mode*. They're playing constant catch-up; they're always behind the curve.

STANDARD THREE: Align Program and Instructional Resources to the Curriculum and Provide Student Equality and Equity

The major resource in schools is *teacher quality time (TQT)* with students. We define TQT as teaching students to be creatively responsive in a deeply aligned curriculum with plenty of opportunities for pedagogical parallelism from the classroom to beyond the tests in use.

In addition, the resources of the school and district must be prioritized to similarly reflect a commitment to improving tested learning, and they must be adjusted so that more resources are diverted to students and programs with greater educational needs than others. School system formulae that level resources to ratios are not effective. They undermine the concept of constancy by shortchanging some children and overspending on others. The idea of *economy of scale* is relative to the needs of the children being considered. What is economical is not a simple arithmetic calculation. It is, rather, needs centered. The idea of adjusting resources to identified needs is that of *equity*.

STANDARD FOUR: Use a Mastery Learning Approach and Effective Teaching Strategies

Mastery learning includes the idea of linking the written and tested curricula with the taught curriculum. It also means that individual learning plans are developed for students who are underachieving. Mastery learning includes instruction at the right level of difficulty for a student. This means that diagnostic assessments are given regularly to ascertain where a student is in his/her learning.

Moreover, there are many well researched, effective teaching practices that when used increase the likelihood of student achievement. It is our expectation that teachers are cognizant of these techniques and use them routinely.

STANDARD FIVE: Establish Curriculum Expectations, Monitoring, and Accountability

This standard relates to the expression of high curriculum standards by administrators but also includes administrative competence in actually monitoring curriculum design and delivery in school classrooms. It means that the principal feels comfortable in working with teachers to disaggregate test data and then use those data to make classroom decisions. Further, it means that district-level officers recognize that their main mission is higher student achievement and that they must also monitor to see if the curriculum is being implemented. Their role in the supervision of principals is essential.

STANDARD SIX: Institute Effective District and School Planning, Staff Development, Resource Allocation, and Provide a Quality Learning Environment

School planning is essential to establish the means for specifying purpose and relating the structure required to attain constancy. Planning must include multiyear goals and determine the requisite change strategies to be employed. On the other hand, plans must retain flexibility and adaptability so that the planning process doesn't promote organizational rigor mortis.

Staff development must be related to the goals contained within school plans. Staff development is not an end unto itself, rather it is a means towards enhancing the human element required to attain organizational ends. As staff becomes more proficient, the school becomes increasingly capable of improving its performance levels.

The school budget is configured by how it is related to curricular priorities. It promotes equity and it supports learning priorities that are established based on need.

Personnel in the school are qualified and motivated. Marginal teachers are brought up to satisfactory standards or encouraged to leave. Crime is minimal and fear is not present. School facilities are adequate, clean, and safe and promote a wide variety of learning and teaching variations in shaping and reshaping an instructional program.

Many school staff members across the nation are floundering in trying to achieve high student success based on student achievement measures. Tremendous amounts of money are spent every year purchasing program after program in an attempt to raise test scores. Many of these efforts prove to be fruitless. Staff members are becoming discouraged and frustrated as they put energy into these programs to no avail. It is time for us to focus our efforts on powerful strategies that research has proven will make a difference.

That is what this book is about. Review the six standards and fifty strategies presented in this book in a diagnostic way, with a view to determining your district's and/or school's present status. At the end of each strategy is a space for you to record your analysis, either for private speculation or for use as a collaborative tool with colleagues or other stakeholders. Ultimately, this book is meant to serve as both a yardstick and a game plan to assist schools in achieving the highest level of performance possible.

1

STANDARD ONE

Establish a Well-Crafted, Focused, Valid and Clear Curriculum to Direct Teaching

The following are nine highly powerful strategies related to curriculum that can be used to achieve higher student achievement:

1. *Ensure External Assessment Target Objectives Are Embedded in the Written Content Standards and Are Linked to State Standards/Expectations*

2. *Have Clear and Precise District Curriculum Objectives- Content, Context, and Cognitive Level*

3. *Deeply Align Objectives from External Assessments*

4. *Sequence Objectives for Mastery Well Before They Are Tested*

5. *Provide a Feasible Number of Objectives to Be Taught*

6. *Identify Specific Objectives as Benchmark Standards*

7. *Place Objectives in a Teaching Sequence*

8. *Provide Access to Written Curriculum Documents and Direct the Objectives to Be Taught*

9. *Conduct Staff Development in Curriculum and Its Delivery*

Strategy 1

Ensure External Assessment Target Objectives Are Embedded in the Written Content Standards and Are Linked to State Standards / Expectations

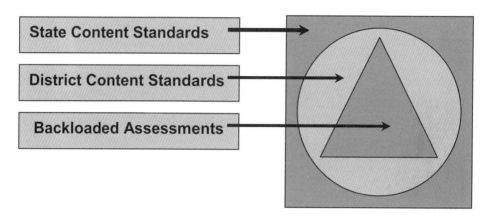

There is a written set of district curriculum content standards that embed all external assessments administered to students and are linked to state standards / expectations for every grade / instructional level and course offered.

Strategy 1: *WHAT*

First and foremost, we must teach that which is assessed. We should embed the tested objectives in the written curriculum goals and objectives. Then, when teachers use these objectives to direct their teaching, there is a high probability students will score well on external tests as well as on your own district assessments.

The mission of the district is defined by the curriculum. A written curriculum is essential to meet the aim of the mission. The mission of a school system is to prepare students to function as effective citizens in our country, to live personally satisfying lives and to contribute to and improve society. The tested curriculum is an important part of the mission and thus must be an essential part of the written curriculum.

Figure 1

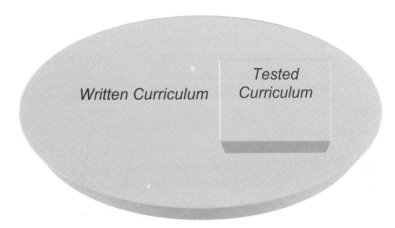

A well-written curriculum provides the content standards (goals) and objectives to be taught.

- Content standards describe the core knowledge, strategies, and skills for schools to teach and for students to acquire and be able to demonstrate *in each subject area.* They describe what students should know and be able to do, as well as the attitudes they will hold after completing an entire program of study.
- Objectives (course or instructional level) describe behaviors in specific terms as to what students will master by the end of a year, semester, or level in a particular area of study.

Content standards need to be linked to state expectations, but most importantly, objectives derived from all external assessments need to form the initial base of the curriculum (*see Figure 1*).

District content standards and objectives need not be directly aligned with the state or national standards; such standards are often too broad and vague to direct teaching, or there are far too many objectives to realistically teach. It is important to select only the most essential and significant objectives to teach. Begin by selecting the tested objectives. Such efforts begin the journey toward a connected and coordinated curriculum delivery.

Strategy 1: *WHY*

If the curriculum fails to include objectives that are ultimately tested, students often will not fare well on the tests. Research is quite clear that students who are heavily dependent upon the schools for their learning such as those who come from lower socioeconomic situations, will typically fail to demonstrate success on the tests unless we teach to them. Surprise, surprise! Students from affluent cultures tend to have extracurricular experiences that are reflected in testing. They will do well on the tests in spite of what is taught in school.

For years teachers have taught whatever *they* thought important. Students learn, but they often do not learn that which is assessed. If students don't have access to information that is tested, then we can't expect them to demonstrate knowledge of the learnings. If a teacher is directed by the textbook curriculum or other instructional resource, it is doubtful that many of the ideas presented in these resources will be tested.

Textbook publishers typically state that they include in the textbook all of the state frameworks and all areas tested. However, in several studies conducted by the authors as well as other researchers, it was discovered that only 30 to 40% of tested objectives were found in textbooks. In one study in an urban school district, the Spanish textbooks addressed just 15% of the objectives tested on the state exam (Houston, 1997).

Strategy 1: *HOW*

Try the following steps to achieve this strategy:

1. Review each test item, if available, on the external test and derive the objective by deconstructing the test item. Deconstructing a test item means identifying what is being taught (the content), and how it is being tested (item format-e.g. multiple choice, bubble in). You may not have access to the actual test items if states are

making these secure tests, but many states provide sample items for practice tests. If your state does not provide items, go to Web pages from several states and review the test items they use. Though the format may vary from that used in your state, the content and testing objectives covered will likely be close enough for the requirements of your state framework.

2. Obtain a different form of the test and deconstruct the test items (if the tests are norm referenced standardized tests).

3. Determine at what grade level the test item is first tested. Often on both state criterion-referenced tests and norm-referenced tests, similar test items will be used at different grades. Analyze the items across grade levels.

4. Identify the frequency with which a given tested objective is tested and the level of difficulty. Norm-referenced test companies frequently provide such information. Be sure to reflect such frequency and difficulty on your practice tests.

5. Place the objectives in content standards. You might want to use the state content standard/framework areas as a tool.

6. Develop a correlation matrix of the tested objectives in relation to the state and/or national standards/frameworks. Be generous in your correlation. Often state officials will want evidence that you are teaching the state standards. File the matrix for legal purposes.

7. Begin the design of the curriculum content standards at each grade level and for each course for the tested subject areas.

Strategy 2

Have Clear and Precise District Curriculum Objectives-Content, Context, and Cognitive Level

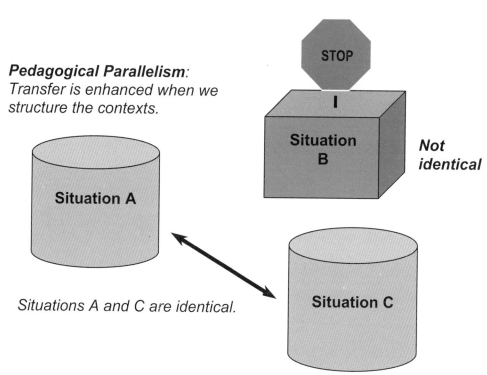

Pedagogical Parallelism: *Transfer is enhanced when we structure the contexts.*

STOP

Situation B

Not identical

Situation A

Situations A and C are identical.

Situation C

The district curriculum objectives, aligned to the external assessment objectives, provide:

- *Clearly specified content (skills, knowledge, attitude, etc.) to be learned;*
- *The context in which the learning must be demonstrated, including the test format;*
- *The appropriate cognitive level to be mastered; and*
- *The standard of performance –the degree of mastery required.*

Strategy 2: WHAT

Design the curriculum so that you teach what is tested (Strategy 1), and then add to that design the *way* it is tested. From a curriculum point of view, this means that the district curriculum needs to be so clear that any teacher will know what to teach and how to practice the learning, as well as how to assess it. State content standards/frameworks are often broad in nature and duplicative across grade levels. A district's curriculum needs to be written to the precise objective level so that there is no question about what will be taught and when.

As mentioned in Strategy 1, objectives for either a course, grade, or instructional level describe in specific behavioral terms what students will be able to do at the end of a year/semester/level in a particular area. Objectives need to be clearly written to minimally include the content to be learned (skill, knowledge, concept, process, attitude, etc.) and the context in which the learning is to be demonstrated.

An objective needs four components to precisely guide teaching:

- **Content:** The topic, concept, process, skill, knowledge, attitude to be learned
- **Context:** The performance conditions under which the student will demonstrate the content
- **Cognitive Level:** The level of thought process required, typically using Bloom's taxonomy (knowledge, comprehension, application, analysis, synthesis, evaluation)
- **Standard of Performance:** The degree to which the students need to show they have mastered the learning.

Most objectives are written with just a vague idea of content and a verb that might indicate the cognitive level of the objective. For example, "Classify objects as acid or alkaline." Just how would one teach to this objective, and how would one know when students have mastered this learning? The content of the objective needs to be more precise. For example, "Classify objects as acid or alkaline substances according to their molecular structure."

Further, the missing piece that really impacts the teacher's planning is the context in which the student is to show he/she knows the content. Context means the conditions or situations in which the student is to demonstrate the learning. There are least three context dimensions:

- Instructional or environmental conditions (what the teacher says; what the directions state; vocabulary needed to learn; level of reading ability required; use of graphs, visuals, and other materials, etc.) These are often called "givens."
- Operation performed or the learner's task requirements (classify, supply information, recall, develop a product).
- Student behavior mode or the physical characteristics of the learner's behavior or product (writing, oral presentation, pointing, circling, filling in an answer, bubbling in a response).

Here is a better example of a written objective: "The student will demonstrate knowledge (cognitive level) of acid and alkali substances as well as their complex molecular structure (content) by writing (context-student mode of response) in order of molecular structure (context-task specifications) 10 chemical substances (context-environmental conditions) correctly on at least three assessments over a 5-month period (standard of performance)."

Because this is difficult to read, sometimes the objective is written this way:

Content: Acid and alkali substances as well as their complex molecular structure

Cognitive Level: Knowledge

Context: Given 10 chemical substances
Put in order of molecular structure
Student will write down the order

Standard of Performance: Correctly on at least three assessments over a seven-month period

What is also presented in the above objective is the standard of performance. Standards of performance are used to judge student achievement at a minimum level of performance. They answer the question "How well must a student perform the behavior to demonstrate mastery?" The performance standard can be quantitative or qualitative in nature. The way the objective is written above is an example of typical practice items in a textbook.

When developing a precise curriculum that ensures sample items from external assessments are backloaded into the curriculum, a "given" of the contexts will have the item format, as exemplified below:

Context:
- Given four chemical substances in four different sequences placed in an (a), (b), (c), (d) format and (e) as "none of the above"
- Student will identify the correct sequence, if presented
- Student will bubble in response

When a district wishes to write a curriculum that moves beyond the external assessments, then multiple contexts will be written. For example, they will use the tested context above, the textbook context (e.g., write the answer), and, hopefully, a real world context such as:

Context:
- Given twenty chemical substances that are households substances
- Place in order of molecular structure
- Write a page for a Household Guide using the district's 5th grade writing rubrics

Figure 2   ***Transfer to Three Types of Situations***

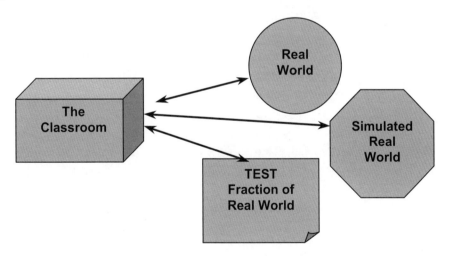

For those of us not willing to have the external assessments comprise the totality of the curriculum, we can then develop contexts that require higher level thought processes needed in real world situations. The way we do this is by changing the cognitive level and the context of the objective.

However, start your curriculum development with the external assessments to get what we call "topological alignment"–a one-to-one match of the test item's content, context and cognitive level requirements.

Strategy 2: WHY

State content standards or frameworks are often broad in nature. Such lack of precision results in teachers teaching the same or similar student learnings across grades and courses. Such nonpurposeful duplication takes time away from the essential learnings.

Providing various contexts in which the teacher has students practice the content of the objective, increases the likelihood that the students will be able to transfer their learning to the various contexts. From study on the transfer of learning (Thorndike) we know that when the pedagogy of the classroom mirrors the situation in which we want the student to demonstrate the content, the student has higher success (see *Figure 2*). One context we want students to transfer their learning to is the external assessment situation. We must teach what is tested (Strategy 1) in the way it is tested and in the context in which it is tested (Strategy 2). When this occurs, we achieve higher measured student achievement on the tests. To attain higher student achievement in multiple situations, we must provide practice and ongoing assessments in many contexts.

Strategy 2: HOW

Try the following steps to achieve this strategy:
1. Complete the steps for Strategy 1.
2. Review each test item from the external assessments, if available, and derive the content and context of the tested objective (by deconstructing the test item). Then determine the cognitive level of the test item (topological alignment). If the tests are norm-referenced standardized tests, obtain a different form of the test and deconstruct the test items.
3. Place these objectives under the derived content standards from Strategy 1.
4. Determine the standard of performance for each objective.
5. Add other contexts as desired, i.e., textbook/instructional resource approach, application or higher cognitive level in a real word context.

Strategy 3

Deeply Align Objectives from External Assessments

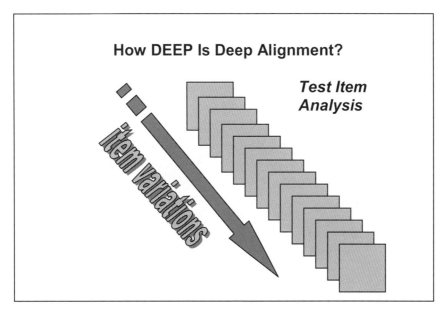

How DEEP Is Deep Alignment?

Test Item Analysis

Item Variations

Objectives based on external assessments are placed (embedded) in the curriculum in a "deeply aligned" manner (content, context, and cognitive level).

Strategy 3: WHAT

The first two strategies are used to design the curriculum so that you teach what is tested (content) and teach it the way it is tested (context). The third strategy is to design the curriculum in a deeply aligned way so that when the objectives are taught students can transfer that learning to a wide variety of situations. Deeply aligned objectives are those that include a broad range of content and contexts. Whether the objective is backloaded from an external assessment or designed in a frontloaded way, it is a process that is essential to help students score well on a test and use the learning in life.

If your district has schools with low-performing scores on state tests, it is absolutely imperative that you deeply backload from the external test. Developing a curriculum for deeper alignment has two major steps. The initial step is to deconstruct the test item and develop curriculum objectives that mirror directly the content, context, and cognitive level of the test item. This is a surface alignment. A teacher, when reading the objective, will know exactly what the test item will look like.

This type of alignment is called *topological alignment*—a one-to-one match of the:

- Content (topic, subject to be learned),
- Context (test situation-conditions under which the students will demonstrate the content), and
- Cognitive level required.

For example, the following is a 5th grade mathematics practice test item used by the State of Florida. This test item uses a gridded response question in which "students must arrive at a numeric answer independently, then write the answer and bubble in the grid."

Figure 3

Florida Sunshine Example—Gridded Response Question

The gymnastics class stood in rows to have their team picture taken. The photographer told 2 people to stand in the first row, 4 people to stand in the second row, and 6 people to stand in the third row.

The photographer continued the pattern. How many people did he tell to stand in the sixth row?

⓪	⓪	⓪	⓪
①	①	①	①
②	②	②	②
③	③	③	③
④	④	④	④
⑤	⑤	⑤	⑤
⑥	⑥	⑥	⑥
⑦	⑦	⑦	⑦
⑧	⑧	⑧	⑧
⑨	⑨	⑨	⑨

Here is what the objective would look like for topological alignment when you deconstruct the test item:

Objective that Has Been Topologically Aligned to the 5th Grade Test Item

Content: Specify the number in a repeated number pattern that requires a skip in the pattern using the simple operations of addition and/or multiplication

Context:

- Given a word problem that is split by a visual depiction of the word problem
- Given a visual depiction that is only part of the problem
- Vocabulary specific to learning that includes ordinal and cardinal numbers, row, continued, pattern
- Student writes answer and then bubbles answer into a number grid

Cognitive Level: Knowledge

Some student gains will be accomplished using topological alignment, but they are minimal. Further, a classroom situation that focuses only on topological alignment can become boring, almost meaningless, unless a teacher understands that this is only one way the learning should be practiced.

However, if you deeply align the objectives in their design from the test item, you begin to provide a curriculum that not only brings meaning to the learning, but that also provides for high achievement on state and national tests. The process for deep alignment involves the following:

- Broadens the content to a reasonable range of learning,
- Expands alternative ways of assessing the content, and
- Moves the cognitive level to higher levels.

The more you move one or more of these three areas, the deeper the alignment. In this type of curriculum design you identify the situations (including various types of test formats) in which you are preparing students to transfer the content learning. This is done so that when teachers teach the content learning, it will be practiced in various contexts and at several cognitive levels. Such practice increases the probability that students will transfer this learning to multiple situations.

This illustration of transfer, first presented in *Strategy 2*, is shown here again in *Figure 4*:

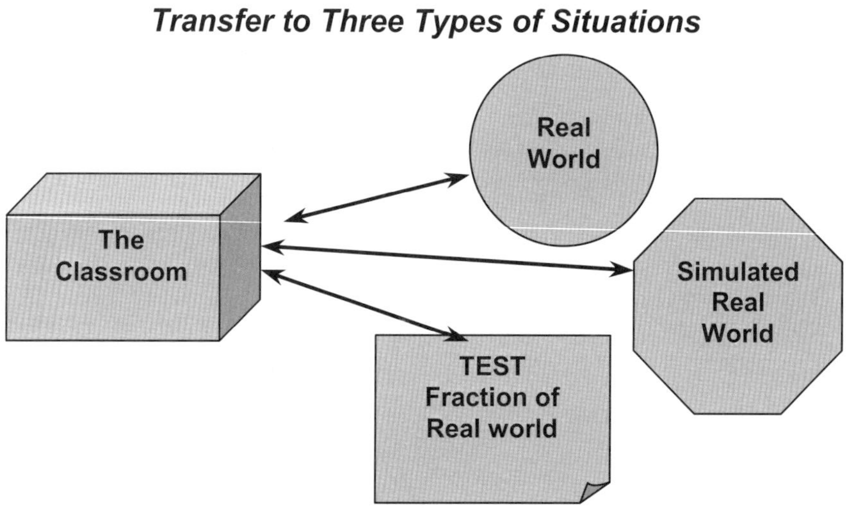

Transfer to Three Types of Situations

Figure 4

The following is an example how you would take the topically aligned objective from the Florida 5th grade test item shown earlier and write it in a deeply aligned way. Italics indicate the changes that move the objective from topical to deep alignment. Note also the additional contexts.

Objective That is Deeply Aligned to the 5th Grade Test Item

Content: Specify the number, *letter,* or *visual symbol* in a repeated number, *letter or visual symbol* pattern that requires a *next in line* and a skip in the pattern using the simple operations of addition and/or multiplication, *subtraction, or division.*

Context 1: *(gridded response)*
- Given a word problem that is split by a visual depiction of the word problem
- Given a visual depiction that is only part of the problem
- Vocabulary which includes ordinal and cardinal numbers, words such as gymnastics, photographer, row, continued, pattern
- Student writes answer and then bubbles answer into a number grid

Cognitive Level	Knowledge

Context 2: *(multiple-choice test)*

- Given a word problem that is split by a visual depiction of the word problem
- Give a visual depiction that is only part of the problem
- Vocabulary which includes ordinal and cardinal numbers and words such as gymnastics, photographer, row, continued, pattern
- Student *selects answer from four possible answers with distracters, most frequent errors, and a "none of the above" answer*
- Student *bubbles correct answer on Scantron-type separate answer sheets*

Cognitive Level:	Knowledge

Context 3: *(multiple-choice test)*

- *Given symbolic pattern*
- *Student selects answer from four possible answers with distracters, most frequent errors, and a "none of the above" answer*
- *Student bubbles correct answer on Scantron-type separate answer sheet*

Cognitive Level:	Knowledge

Context 4: *(typical textbook approach)*

- *Given symbolic pattern, student writes in answer and explains the answer*

Cognitive Level:	Comprehension

Context 5: *(real-world pattern simulation, requiring student to show reasoning, per writing objective)*

- *Given a word problem depicting a real world situation*
- *Given a direction to determine a pattern*
- *Student writes the pattern and a descriptive paragraph explaining the reasoning behind the correct answer*
- *Paragraph must meet 5th grade writing rubric*

Cognitive Level:	Application

Strategy 3: WHY

Deep alignment provides for a maximization of design and, subsequently, classroom delivery parallelism and, therefore, learning. Educators should maximize the pedagogical and environmental congruence between teaching and the various testing situations a student might experience as well as provide the real use of the learning.

Deep alignment is based on Edward L. Thorndike's concept of *transfer*. Transfer is enhanced when the situational contexts are similar. Thorndike called his idea "the identical element theory" of the transfer of learning. When students practice and learn a skill, knowledge, concept, or process in a certain way, they should be able to transfer the learning to a similar situation. Since there are many ways a student will be challenged to use the learning in school and out, we must practice it in as many of those contexts as possible.

A deeply aligned curriculum and its delivery provide exceptionally high gains in student achievement. When you think about this, it is common sense. If you practice a learning to mastery in many different ways, you increase the probability that you can successfully use the learning in many ways. When a deeply aligned curriculum is delivered, such learnings take on more meaning for students as well. One of the things we have often noticed in our classroom observations is that much learning is not being taught in a real-world way. We strongly advocate and emphasize that one of the contexts you transfer learning to be a real-world situation.

Strategy 3: HOW

Try the following steps to achieve this strategy, after having accomplished the steps in Strategies 1 and 2:

1. Use a deconstructed objective (content, context, cognitive level) and a test item from Strategy 2 to develop a revised objective by broadening the content, by writing various real-world contexts and by changing the cognitive level as desired.
2. Add more contexts to reflect the way you want the learning tested within the district and include contexts that will allow for higher cognitive levels and more authentic assessments.

We highly recommend that no objective be written without the contexts, nor without writing at least one district sample test item for each of the contexts identified (see Strategy 10).

Strategy 4

Sequence Objectives for Mastery Well Before They Are Tested

Objectives are placed in the sequence of learning at least six months to one year before the students must first demonstrate mastery on the external test.

Strategy 4: WHAT

It is important that students have the opportunity to learn well that which is tested. "Learn well" means that a student has mastered the learning or can go beyond mere recall with the learned facts or concepts and apply them in a variety of contexts and at challenging cognitive levels. Many times student learning does not progress beyond the simple memorization of facts, figures, or concepts, and the application of the same in limited contexts. We want our instructional practice to move past "surface" learning; students' knowledge is useless if it cannot be quickly and efficiently recalled to be used in classroom and real-life situations. This strategy deals with changing instructional practice to better facilitate learning of skills, facts, and concepts, and to then provide students with enough time to apply that learning in new and challenging situations (contexts). The application of the content needs to take place over time, ideally a full six months to a year before the content is tested, while giving the students intermittent reinforcement.

Strategy 4 is accomplished in two ways: sequencing the learning objectives so they are mastered well in advance of being tested, and including the standard of performance within an objective. One of the reasons for including the standard of performance in an objective is to provide teachers with an idea of what constitutes mastering the content. This involves the point at which a student not only has committed the learning to memory, but can also recall and use the information in many different situations, including a testing situation. For instance, in the example dealing with acid and alkaline provided on page 14 of this book, the following was the standard of performance: "Correctly on at least three assessments over a seven-month period."

Strategy 4: WHY

When a student is held accountable on a test for a particular learning, it is only fair that student has had the opportunity to master that learning in advance of the testing situation and has had adequate time in which to apply that learning in various contexts (practice). When designing the curriculum, many district staff members, place an objective into the curriculum the same year it is tested externally. However, objectives need to be placed in the curriculum earlier so students have adequate time to demonstrate mastery. The standard of performance is the gauge by which teachers can determine if mastery has been reached.

Students across the country, good students, are "cramming for the test." Yet a year later they remember little that they learned, because the practice of that learning occurred during a few long study sessions. This is referred to as "massed practice." In contrast, when students are given more time to learn material and additional opportunities to practice that material (distributed practice), they are more likely to retain their learning and use it in future situations, including testing situations *(Woolfolk, 1987).*[3]

Our premise here is that we must decide on the important learnings and provide students with adequate opportunities to acquire the learnings and apply them in multiple situations and problems. Further, if these learnings are tested in advance, this will also allow teachers and students the time and practice necessary to master the test situation and question formats.

One of the nice side effects of placing objectives in a teaching sequence well before the objectives are tested is that the curriculum becomes more challenging. However, we

---

Woolfolk, Anita E. (1987). *Educational Psychology.* Englewood Cliffs, NJ: Prentice-Hall, Inc.

will have to be careful to make sure that the instructional resources and textbooks we use are aligned to the curriculum (see Strategy 22).

Strategy 4: HOW

Try the following steps to achieve this strategy:

1. Review the tested objectives and then locate that objective in the curriculum at least six months to a year earlier in the scope and sequence of learning.
2. Examine norm-referenced test planning documents to determine where the objective is first tested. Most objectives are tested over more than a two to three year span.
3. Sequence the objectives in the scope in such a way that teachers have plenty of time to move students to mastery.
4. Create a scope matrix across grades so teachers can see when the student is to learn (master) the objective and when it is tested (*see Figure 5*).

Figure 5

Sample Scope Matrix

Content Objective	Level											
	K	1	2	3	4	5	6	7	9	10	11	12
Identify ordinal numbers												
	M	D	S									
Count, recognize, represent, name, order, and write whole numbers												
Up to 99 (not write in words)	M D											
Up to 999 (not write in words)		M D	S									
Up to 9,999			M D S	D S	S							
Up to 99,999				M D		S						
Up to 999,999,999					M D		S		E			
Estimate numbers including ordinal, time, temperature, miles, and money												
Up to 99	M											
Up to 999		M										
Up to 9,999			M	S	S							
Up to 99,999				M			S					
Up to 999,999,999 and two-place decimals						M S			E			
KEY:												
M = Year in which the objective is to be MASTERED												
D = District Assessments (Pre/Post and Probes)												
S = State Assessment												
E = State Exit Exam												

5. Create a Matrix showing where in each grade/level/course each objective is to be mastered (See Strategy 10).

6. Choose not to use a scope matrix with the terms *introduce, develop, and master*. Such terms have little meaning for teachers and provide an avenue for them not to be held accountable for student learning in an area.

Strategy 5

Provide a Feasible Number of Objectives to Be Taught

There is a feasible number of objectives to be learned so that students can master them. A time range for each is noted. District time allocations for all subject areas/courses are in place from which to compare feasibility.

Strategy 5: WHAT

Less is more, as the saying goes. Fewer objectives taught in depth have a higher probability of being remembered. It is important that a district curriculum, in its design, has a feasible number of objectives that can be taught to mastery. A district needs to identify the most essential skills to be taught to students and that students are expected to master. When we estimate the time needed to not only acquire the learning (short-term memory), but also to master the learning (long-term memory), we must limit the number of objectives taught.

Identifying the most essential skills is easy to mandate but difficult to do. What students should learn is based upon opinion. We have the opinions of national experts, state committees, and test makers as to what are the most important learnings. Certainly you need to include as essential those learnings a student will be held accountable for through assessments. And, if we could influence you, we would include real-world learnings such as those shown in the SCANS Report.

When we teach to mastery, we provide numerous practice opportunities over several months in order for the student to retain the learning. The range of time needed to master an objective varies greatly depending upon the complexity and meaning of the learning. For example, learning one's ABCs takes rote memorization, while learning how to write an expository paragraph with certain elements requires a synthesis of ideas, and, therefore, greater time to master.

Curriculum designers need to give objectives a best estimate of time-not only time for a typical student to acquire the learning, but also the time needed to retain the learning. For example, if we have a 10 to 15 hour range of time per objective and have 150 hours available in a year for the learning, it is easy to see that we could work with no more than 10 to 15 objectives per year in a given subject area.

Design a curriculum around the typical learner and ensure that there are not too many objectives to be taught. Develop the curriculum around instructional levels rather than grade levels. This will allow the student to advance to the next level of objectives when ready and also stay with his or her age mates. This is a concept known as "continuous progress." This approach works in conjunction with the differentiation of instruction described in Strategy Thirty. Each student is moved along the continuum of learning objectives at a challenging and appropriate learning pace.

Strategy 5: WHY

It is time to be reasonable. We hand a teacher one hundred plus objectives to teach in a 150-hour period of time and then wonder why the students haven't mastered the objectives. It is no wonder voluminous curriculum guides with hundreds of objectives sit on shelves, and teachers, when receiving the state standards, sigh. It's wrong. It's ridiculous. Why does such nonsense persist? It's very understandable why teachers turn to their textbooks and start with page 1. However, textbooks have far too many objectives as well, and their alignment to the tested objectives is usually very poor (see Strategy 22).

Some people call it "March Madness." But this madness happens any time teachers begin to realize that there is no way that they can cover all the objectives they have been told to teach by the end of the year. Some teachers, under pressure, begin to skim even more quickly over some objectives, with the result that students lose opportunities to remember the learnings of the objectives. The same thing happens if teaching is textbook driven. This is illogical.

While the number of curriculum objectives in the United States is growing, countries whose students are obtaining the highest scores on international tests are teaching fewer objectives but with greater depth. How could it be that fewer objectives are taught, but students remember more? It comes back to the concept of practice as discussed in Strategy 3, teaching for a deeper understanding of content versus rote memorization.

A feasible number of objectives means we have a higher probability that the students will learn what we want them to learn. This strategy works hand in hand with Strategy 4- design curriculum so that teachers teach the learning well in advance of it being tested. When you have a doable number of objectives and students are learning the skills to mastery, you have a high probability that not only will the students do well on tests, but that they will also remember the knowledge, skill, concept, or process for use in life.

One of the complaints we often hear from teachers is that their students do not have the prerequisite skills expected. In most cases, this is attributed to the fact that students are not learning the knowledge or skills taught in the previous grade to mastery. When there are too many objectives to be taught, the teachers just move from one objective to the next without allowing for the practice opportunities needed to obtain retention of the learning.

Because students of low-performing schools are often disadvantaged with respect to the areas taught, limiting the objectives gives them an equal opportunity to score well on external assessments. Why is it test scores float on demographics? It is not because students from certain demographics are smarter than others, obviously. One contributing factor is the major difference in experiences students bring to the testing situation, experiences that occur outside of the school setting. Giving students access to the learnings for which they are going to be held accountable on tests means we have to be smart about the number of objectives we are going to place in the curriculum for teachers to teach.

Further, we need to make sure that the learnings students will be held accountable for are in the curriculum. In no way would this limit the teaching of other objectives once the externally tested objectives are mastered.

Strategy 5: HOW

Try the following steps to achieve this strategy:

1. Identifying the tested objectives and embed them in the curriculum.
2. Specifying the content, context, and cognitive level of each objective.
3. Broaden the range of the content, context, and cognitive level of each objective), and
4. Place the objectives early in the learning sequence before testing externally.

The steps are:

a. Establish Curriculum Time Allocations–the amount of instructional time to be devoted to each subject area/course for every grade level. For example:

Grade Level	Subject Area	Time Allocation Daily
2	Language Arts (Including SSR)	150 minutes (15 minutes)
	Mathematics	90 minutes
	Social Studies	90 minutes 3 times a week
	Science	90 minutes 2 times a week
	Physical Education/Health	50 minutes 2 times every six days
	Music	50 minutes 2 times every six days
	Art	50 minutes 2 times every six days

b. Determine a probable range of time for each objective for a typical student to learn it to mastery-estimate the amount of acquisition time and practice time needed for retention of the learning.

c. Total up the number of hours for a subject area/course in a given semester or year.

d. Compare the number of hours to teach the objectives you want to teach with the number of available instructional hours. You have too many, right? Now that you have found that you don't have enough time, eliminate some of the objectives (the hard part). Eliminate last those areas tested most frequently.

e. Work across grade levels as this project is accomplished since more time may be found at other grade levels. Remember to place an objective where it is first tested, not in every grade in which it is tested.

f. Publish the content standards and objectives for teachers, parents, and students.

It is recognized that learning can and does take place in an integrated way in school. A student learns more about reading in social studies and uses more math skills in science. Our approach to determining the number of objectives is linear, yet we expect integrated teaching. However, we have found that when you complete Strategy Five in a subject-specific way, you get closer to a feasible number of objectives. If teachers find they have more time to teach more objectives than required, they should move along the continuum of objectives.

Strategy 6

Identify Specific Objectives as Benchmark Standards

Some of the objectives have been identified as district benchmark standards to be used as feedback for learning progress, program value, curriculum redesign, promotion, etc.

Strategy 6: WHAT

A benchmark is a milestone you are trying to reach. Benchmark standards serve as milestones for a particular level of learning–a goal to be attained. Benchmarks should be a sampling of the curriculum objectives that could be used to ascertain accomplishment of learnings in a group of grades, a program, or a curriculum.

Typically, these district benchmarks are for grade spans, such as at the end of grades 3, 6, 9, and 11. They often are set a year in advance of any state benchmark testing. Since we suggest that any objective tested be placed early in the sequence of learning (see Strategy Four), it makes sense that the district benchmarks would be a year earlier than the state benchmark assessments.

Some districts are beginning to develop benchmark standards for every year due to annual high-stakes testing. Whatever you do must, in part, be determined by the consequences of students not performing well on state and national assessments. Recently, benchmark standards have been required by states as a means to determine retention of students in a grade. This makes placement of learnings early in the curriculum even more critical to ensure that no student is retained.

The frequency at which benchmarks are assessed will depend on how you plan to use the information. Hopefully, it will not be for retention of students in grades, but rather to ensure promotion to the next grade of all students and for program and curriculum decision-making. In the latter situation, only a random sampling of students need be assessed.

There are two types of benchmark standards:

- Benchmark content/objective standards
- Benchmark performance standards

They go hand and in hand. The first is what we want students to learn; the second is how we will measure that learning. To better define them:

Benchmark Content Standards and Objectives are those selected student objectives that will serve as a summative point at certain times in the schooling of a student. They describe what students will know or be able to do, or attitudes they will hold after completing an entire program of study or groups of years/courses.

Benchmark Performance Standards state the evidence required to document attainment of the benchmark content standard and/or objective, and the quality of student performance deemed acceptable (e.g., mastered, or a rubric of advanced, proficient, basic, fail levels).

For more information on performance benchmark standards see Strategy 11.

Strategy 6: WHY

This strategy is difficult to discuss because much of the public debate surrounding benchmarks centers on the belief that students should be retained in a grade if they have not mastered a certain set of learnings. Research is quite clear about the negative impact of retaining students.

Students should not be penalized because we have not taught them successfully. Benchmarks need to be used to assist us in helping students, not in punishing them. You will need to be principled about your beliefs in this arena. The century's worth of research in this area is irrefutable. Further, you will need to set up both a design and delivery of curriculum that will increase the likelihood that students who might not reach the benchmarks are identified early, so that an intensive approach to student promotion is in place. In some ways, the focus on retention in so many states moves us to do the work we should have been doing anyway–providing high success for all students in their achievement.

Our approach to benchmarks in this strategy is not for the purpose of retaining students in school. Rather, it is to underscore that educators should have expectations of learning–goals to be accomplished. These benchmarks may be used to determine the effectiveness of our programs, our curriculum, and our educators.

If we use benchmarks in a data-gathering approach to help us improve, they will help us determine when we need to revise the curriculum or make it more challenging. Benchmarks can be used to set school improvement goals, faculty goals, and personal student achievement goals.

Strategy 6: HOW

Try the following steps to implement this strategy after accomplishing the steps for Strategies 1 through 6:

1. Peruse the objectives to determine which of all of the objectives you will use as benchmark standards.
2. Use those state and national high-stakes assessed objectives that are most frequently tested and that typically should have been mastered prior to a specific grade level.
3. Establish retention benchmark standards that are mainly from the previous grade. This prevents penalizing a student. Yet, expect the grade level benchmarks for assessing educator success.
4. Revise the benchmarks as students learn.
5. Publish the benchmark objectives for teachers, parents, and students.

Strategy 7

Place Objectives in a Teaching Sequence

The objectives are developed in a teaching sequence rather than in the order of state standard/framework strands and are presented to teachers in this same manner.

Strategy 7: WHAT

Once the objectives have been identified, it is important to put them in some logical sequence-the order in which the objectives are to be taught. For years curriculum designers thought there were a tremendous number of dependencies from one learning to another. Through testing this belief it has been established that most learnings have few dependencies-one learning required before another. For example, for many years it was thought that addition and subtraction needed to be taught before multiplication and division. We have now found that this is not the case. These basic mathematical operations can be taught in a variety of sequences.

However, it is still important to put the objectives in some sort of acquisition and maintenance sequence for teachers. The first sequencing of objectives needs to be tied to state and national tests and when curriculum designers want mastery to be achieved (see Strategy 4). After that, a logical approach can be used.

We would suggest educators follow the typical sequence in a textbook. But don't suggest the teacher tackle all the objectives in a textbook or other instructional resource;

this would far exceed what is feasible (see Strategy 5). If, however, it is feasible, there is less skipping around.

In addition to sequencing the learning early, it is important to sequence the objectives across grade or instructional levels. Such sequencing provides for connectivity from one type of objective to another but also provides for the increasing complexity of a concept through a spiraling type of approach.

Strategy 7: WHY

Most state standards or frameworks are built around strands, e.g., number sense. One shouldn't teach an entire strand of a subject area and then move onto another strand. Rather, teach multiple strands at the same time. If teachers don't provide the sequence of objectives, it leaves this decision to teachers. Such a decision can increase the probability of a disjointed and fragmented delivery of the objectives. Further, such a decision would not provide for the integration of objectives across disciplines when students have multiple teachers.

Sequencing the objectives in the order they tend to show up in a textbook helps teachers become aware that they are not to teach everything in the textbook. We could gradually move teachers away from being textbook driven by such an approach. We also increase the possibility of connectivity from one teacher to another in the same grade and the consistency in teaching the same course throughout a district.

Coordination means that the student has access to the same curriculum when in the same course or grade/instructional level, regardless of the school or teacher. For instance, in one school district there were eleven teachers of U.S. History. The course catalog across the high schools had the same course title and course description. However, when the objectives were examined, eleven electives were found. The objectives were not the same–there was minimal coordination in place.

Moreover, the sequence of objectives needs to be designed in an articulated way from one grade to another. This vertical alignment is known as *articulation* and it provides a flow or sequence from one objective to the next. Providing this articulation increases the likelihood of coordination or horizontal alignment as the curriculum is delivered.

You need to decide how much vertical articulation and horizontal coordination you are going to have. These concepts are illustrated in *Figure 6*.

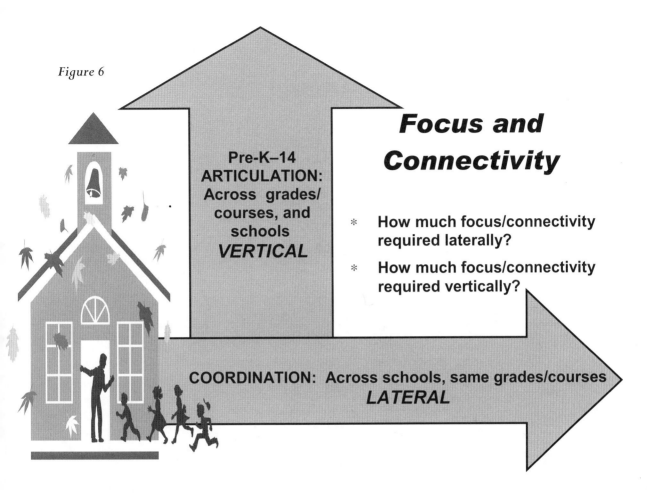

Figure 6

Pre-K–14
ARTICULATION:
Across grades/
courses, and
schools
VERTICAL

Focus and Connectivity

* **How much focus/connectivity required laterally?**

* **How much focus/connectivity required vertically?**

COORDINATION: Across schools, same grades/courses
LATERAL

Strategy 7: HOW

Try the following steps to achieve this strategy:

1. Place the objectives in a logical teaching sequence once they have been decided upon.
2. Build into the sequence both acquisition and mastery practice expectations. Some describe this as a type of curriculum mapping, although the formal term *curriculum mapping* has a much greater meaning in educational literature–a type of gap analysis between what is being taught and what is supposed to be taught.
3. Sequence all objectives across grade or instructional levels and across courses.
4. Place the results in a matrix and indicate a probable timetable based on the probable time needed to master the objective based on the typical student (see Strategy 5).

Strategy 8

Provide Access to Written Curriculum Documents and Direct the Objectives to Be Taught

The school-based administrators and teachers have in their possession current curriculum and instructional documents (e.g., scopes and sequences, course of studies, guides) for all curricular areas. Policy directs teachers to teach to the objectives and administrators to monitor their implementation.

Strategy 8: WHAT

A simple step not often taken in school districts is ensuring that all the users of the curriculum have access to it. This means not only should teachers and other educators have access to the curriculum, but the principals and other site-based administrators should have this access as well. All teachers must have the scope and sequences of objectives for every subject and every grade. These need to be located in each written curriculum document.

However, staff members also need copies of matrixes of aligned resources and assessments for areas they do not teach. Each school and district office should have a professional library so teachers have access to the curriculum taught by other staff members. As curriculum is placed on-line, access becomes even easier.

Documents need to be available for students and parents as well. The scope and sequence of learning objectives needs to be on the district Web page and also on the school Web page.

A second point in Strategy 8 is determine and direct curriculum, assessment, and instructional expectations. It is essential that staff understand that the curriculum is the mission of the school. The curriculum is the very work plan of the organization. Assessments must be aligned to the curriculum and teachers are to teach the curriculum. This is illustrated in *Figure 7*:

Figure 7

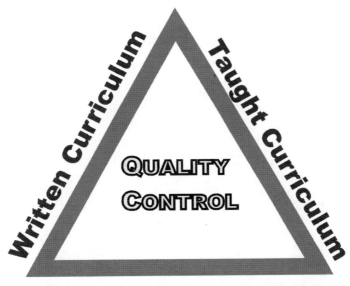

Curriculum: The work plan
Teaching: The work
Assessment: The work measure

To ensure the alignment of the curriculum, teaching, and assessment, the following directive statements should appear in either district board policy or administrative regulations:

- An aligned written, tested, and taught curriculum
- Board adoption of the curriculum
- Accountability through roles and responsibilities
- Written curriculum for all subject/learning areas

- Periodic review of the curriculum
- Textbook/resource alignment to curriculum and assessment
- Program integration and alignment to curriculum
- Vertical articulation and horizontal coordination
- Training for staff in the delivery of the curriculum
- Delivery of the curriculum by teachers
- Monitoring of the delivery of the curriculum by principals
- Equitable student access to the curriculum
- A student and program assessment plan
- Use of data from assessment to determine program and curriculum effectiveness
- Resource allocation tied to curriculum priorities
- Data driven decisions for the purpose of increasing student learning

Moreover, it needs to be clear which curriculum design decisions should be system based 9at the district level) and which should be school based.

Figure 8

TIGHTLY HELD	**LOOSELY HELD**
System-based	*School-based*
• Ends	• Means
• Mission	• Instruction
• Standards	• Strategies
• Goals and priorities	• Groupings
• Student objectives	• Staffing
• Student assessments	• Processes
	• Resources/Textbooks

In this table, the curriculum—what we want students to learn—and its assessment are district responsibilities. These can be decided collaboratively, but they are nonnegotiable once determined. How the curriculum is delivered could be a school, grade, department, or even teacher decision. Before a district moves to this division of responsibility, however, a focused, precise set of learning objectives must be in place along with locally aligned assessments (see Strategies 10, 11, and 12).

In addition, the roles and responsibilities of staff regarding the design and delivery of the curriculum need to be in place. These directives should be obvious through job descriptions, appraisal processes, and student progress reports.

A third critical point in this strategy is to develop a format of the curriculum that is easy for users to understand. Provide a menu of ways users could access the information based upon their preferences. Some teachers, for instance, will only want the scope and sequence of objectives. Other staff members will want example assessment items and time frames. Some staff members may want all of the above plus information regarding aligned resources (see Strategy 22)

Strategy 8: WHY

Typically, staff members will have access to the curriculum when it is initially rolled out. But as the curriculum evolves, the revisions are not provided in a systematic way to staff. Further, new staff coming on board in later years are sometimes not given the documents. It is amazing how many school districts have not provided teachers with copies of the district's curriculum documents. Teachers often report that they requested these documents several times and then gave up.

Our observations are that principals and other school-based administrators rarely have complete copies of the curriculum in their offices. Further, most school-based administrators have little or no knowledge of the curriculum. It is essential that those supervising the work, know the work. Most senior officers do not expect this requirement of their administrative core.

In examining board policy and administrative regulations, we came across volumes of directives, but few focused on the mission of the organization. Seldom do we come across directives requiring a written curriculum. Further, policies are weak on aligned assessment expectations. Most policies do not require teachers to teach the curriculum. Policies or administrative regulations need to clearly spell out the responsibilities of curriculum, assessment, and instruction.

Job descriptions are often weak in setting up competencies regarding curriculum and its implementation. Teacher appraisal systems often fail to include the expectation that teachers are to teach the curriculum. Principal evaluation systems infrequently include the responsibility of monitoring the curriculum. (For more ideas see Strategy 39).

Student progress reports and grade reports rarely include the student objectives to be learned; rather, they call for a vague report on a few areas and for a grade.

Lastly, it is important to provide the curriculum and supporting information to teachers in a form that they will use. One-size-fits-all is not a rational approach. Discussions with the users of the curriculum will tell you what they want.

Strategy 8: HOW

Try the following steps to achieve this strategy:

1. Write and adopt polices and/or approve administrative regulations that direct the design of the written curriculum, philosophical design parameters, assessment expectations, and the expectation that teachers teach the curriculum and principals monitor its use.

2. Review job descriptions of all educators to ascertain if critical competencies regarding the curriculum and its implementation are included. Revise the job descriptions as needed.

3. Examine the teacher and principal appraisal systems to ensure that there are expectations regarding the teaching and monitoring of the curriculum.

4. Design student progress reports around the curriculum objectives as well as a specified grade.

5. Set up a process to ensure that every instructional staff member has access to a complete and current set of curriculum documents.

6. Develop a menu of ways the curriculum can be packaged to assist users in its implementation.

Strategy 9

Conduct Staff Development in Curriculum And in Its Delivery

School-based staff members receive quality training in the curriculum scope and sequence and in the use of curriculum documents.

Strategy 9: WHAT

This is a common-sense strategy. Unfortunately, most districts don't even come close to providing the training necessary to prepare teachers and other staff to understand the need for a curriculum, its design, and the expectations and strategies for its implementation.

Here are some initial ideas for minimal training you need to consider:

- If you embark on a curriculum development effort, the individuals selected for this design task must have the skills needed to perform this function.

- Designers need to understand the various audiences that will use the curriculum and the various ways of packaging the curriculum, including an on-line curriculum for parent, student, teacher, and community member use.
- Attitudinal training is needed to ensure that teachers have a commitment to teaching the curriculum.
- Training in how the curriculum was designed and the philosophical underpinnings of its design, including alignment, is essential.
- Once the curriculum is designed, teachers, administrators, instructional aides, and other educators need to know how to enter the curriculum and how to review and use the various curriculum documents available.
- Decision-making strategies for how to implement the curriculum are absolutely imperative for teachers in ensuring the curriculum is taught.

It is critical that the curriculum design trainers recognize approaches to adult learning and establish a learning community environment. The Curriculum Management Improvement Model Criteria are as follows:

- Provides for organizational, unit, and individual development in a systemic manner.
- Is based on a careful analysis of data and is data driven.
- Focuses on proven research-based approaches that have proved to increase productivity.
- Provides for three phases of the change process: initiation, implementation, and institutionalization.
- Is based on human learning and development as well as adult learning.
- Uses a variety of staff development approaches.
- Provides the follow-up and on-the-job application necessary to ensure improvement.
- Requires an evaluation process that is ongoing, includes multiple sources of information, focuses on all levels of the organization, and is based on actual cases of changed behavior.

Strategy 9: WHY

Most curriculum is designed in a hurried way over the summer using well-meaning people who, with little or no training, attempt to design a complex curriculum in a short period of time. The result is, in almost all cases, a curriculum that is typically:

- Misaligned to state and national testing scenarios
- Poorly written (goals and objectives have little precision)
- Fragmented and often duplicative

- Haphazardly articulated across grades and courses
- Overstuffed with too many objectives to be addressed within the time frame available.

To write a clear, valid, and aligned curriculum requires technical curriculum writing skills. It is imperative that the curriculum designers either have the skills or are trained in the skills to carry out the task. Certainly, minimally, the individuals need to be analytical people with a broad understanding of the learnings across grades and disciplines. The ability to write objectives, spiral these objectives across the grades, and write aligned assessments are basic skill requirements.

Designers need to consider the various audiences who will be using the curriculum and design user-friendly curriculum documents for them. What will parents want to know? How will students use the knowledge of what they are to learn? How will teachers understand the relationship between what they are accountable to teach in relation to what other teachers are teaching? Establishing these essential questions is a first step in this process.

We have found that in most of the schools we've visited across the country, staff members are seldom committed to teaching the district curriculum. Rather, staff members are textbook-committed. This is in part because educators have not focused on the need for a curriculum and required that it be followed. Training in the why of the curriculum, its philosophical framework, and the need to follow it must take place before ever putting the curriculum in the hands of staff members.

We don't want doorstop curriculum; rather, we want a living and dynamic curriculum in place. There are so many reasons for teachers to use the curriculum, it would take several pages to present them, but three of the most pressing reasons we would bring to your attention are the need to:

- Focus teaching on the most essential learnings, including those tested by the state or other external agencies, so that students have the opportunity to thoroughly learn ideas that will be tested.
- Connect learnings to provide a smooth flow for students across multiple teachers and to ensure students have the prerequisite learnings needed from grade to grade.
- Provide equal access to the same continuum of learning objectives even though these may be delivered in different ways. It is the right of the student to have equal access to as well as equal success with individualized strategies.

Unfortunately, many staff members do not have this commitment, for a variety of reasons. Teaching staff are for the most part good people working hard every day. We need to provide them the training opportunities to achieve the expectation that faculty are not individual entrepreneurs but rather employees of the system expected to deliver the planned curriculum. The K-12 public schools should not be a place academic freedom prevails.

After the curriculum is designed and staff members have a commitment to teach, provide training in its use. Training staff members in how to house and manage the curriculum documents-whether on-line, on a disk, or via hard copy-is critical; after this train teachers in the various ways they can use the documents to direct their teaching.

Strategy 9: HOW

Try the following steps to achieve this strategy:
1. List all the various audiences who will need training in the curriculum and the purposes of the training.
2. Specify the competencies needed for the various audiences and purposes.
3. Establish ways to diagnose the various competencies to differentiate the staff members development opportunities.
4. Design evaluation processes to provide feedback on the improvements of the training design as well as to assess individual proficiencies after training.
5. Develop the training opportunities around the National Staff Development Council Standards.
6. Set up the timing of the training to provide staff members a minimum of six months to prepare before they are to use the curriculum.
7. Implement the training and evaluate it.

ℂℛ *Analysis of Standard One* ℰ⍵

Now it is time for you to evaluate the status of your school or school district on Standard One: *Establish a Well-Crafted, Focused, Valid, and Clear Curriculum to Direct Teaching*. For each strategy think about the current status of your situation with regard to these strategies and whether the status is adequate or not. Then determine what changes are needed to meet the criteria of Standard One. Use the spaces below to record your observations.

STRATEGY	CURRENT STATUS	CHANGES NEEDED
1. Ensure External Assessment Target Objectives are Embedded in the Written Content Standards and Are Linked to State Standards/ Expectations	❑Adequate ❑Not adequate	
2. Have Clear and Precise District Curriculum Objectives-Content, Context, and Cognitive Level	❑Adequate ❑Not adequate	
3. Deeply Align Objectives from External Assessments	❑Adequate ❑Not adequate	
4. Sequence Objectives for Mastery Well Before They Are Tested	❑Adequate ❑Not adequate	
5. Provide a Feasible Number of Objectives to Be Taught	❑Adequate ❑Not adequate	
6. Identify Specific Objectives as Benchmark Standards	❑Adequate ❑Not adequate	
7. Place Objectives in a Teaching Sequence	❑Adequate ❑Not adequate	
8. Provide Access to Written Curriculum Documents and Direct the Objectives to Be Taught	❑Adequate ❑Not adequate	
9. Conduct Staff Development in Curriculum and Its Delivery	❑Adequate ❑Not adequate	

2

STANDARD TWO

Provide Assessments Aligned to the Curriculum

The following are nine powerful strategies regarding the assessment process that can be used to achieve high student achievement:

10. Develop Aligned District Pre/Post Criterion-Referenced Assessments

11. Have a Pool of Unsecured Test Items for Each Objective

12. Establish Secured Performance Benchmark Assessments

13. Conduct Assessment Training

14. Use Assessments Diagnostically

15. Teach Students to Be "Test Wise"

16. Establish a Reasonable Testing Schedule and Environment

17. Disaggregate Assessment Data

18. Maintain Student Progress Reports

Strategy 10

Develop Aligned District Pre/Post Criterion-Referenced Assessments

For each objective there are aligned, criterion-referenced assessment items–both content and context. From these items the district has secure district-level, pre/post assessments aligned to each district objective and the external assessments. Practice assessments are also available. All assessment items for each objective are equivalent/parallel. These tests will be given to students at the appropriate instructional level.

Strategy 10: WHAT

This strategy begins very reminiscent of strategies 1-9. Strategy 10 refines the definitions and uses of context and content alignment. Student assessment has always been an integral part of the classroom teaching process. Teachers regularly assess students to determine what they have learned. These assessments generally take place at the end of a unit, chapter, or semester. They provide teachers with valuable information that informs their instructional planning for the next sequence.

As discussed earlier, by reviewing test results, teachers know which students are mastering the objectives and which students need more practice. With this information subsequent instruction can be designed to remediate those areas of deficiency and bring all students up to a level of proficiency deemed necessary by the teacher. *Figure 9* depicts this sequence. The sequence is repeated again and again throughout the school year.

This sequence of planning, teaching, testing, and reviewing results needs to be applied to the broader context of state accountability assessment. Moreover, it's important that we not just look at the model as a teach-and-test approach but as a plan-test-teach-test-reteach type approach as well. This will be elaborated in Strategy 28: *Implement a Mastery Learning Model* and is exemplified as follows.

Figure 9

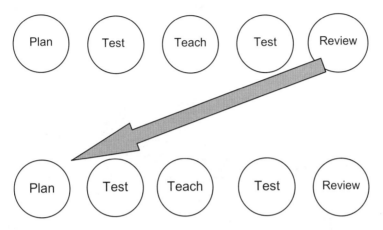

Strategy 10: WHY

There is an old adage: "Students do better on tests if you teach them what you test than if you don't." It is common sense to be sure that students are taught the material on which they are tested. This is just as true for state accountability assessments as it is for classroom assessments.

These assessments must include both content and context alignment. Content alignment refers to the subject matter being assessed. If students are to be tested on two-digit multiplication, then they should be taught two-digit multiplication. Most published state frameworks describe the content goals and objectives that are to be assessed on the state exam. Context alignment refers to the format of the assessment. Typical classroom assessments include true/false, completion, and short essay responses. Students become familiar with these types of assessments and are not surprised when faced with them. On the other hand, students may not be familiar with multiple choice assessments or open-ended response items. If the first time a students sees this type of assessment is on the state test, the lack of familiarity may prevent the student from answering correctly and not allow the student to display the knowledge he or she possesses.

Teachers should think of the state and other external assessment systems as graphic organizers for their teaching. The state curriculum framework becomes the content taught (similar to a teaching unit), the state assessment becomes the measure of how well students learned the content (similar to the end-of-unit test), and the lessons teachers plan enable students to learn the material. It is taking what is already common practice in classrooms and expanding it to a broader arena.

By constructing a pre- and post-test assessment system that is aligned with the state framework and assessment system, classroom teachers are simply following the good pedagogy they currently understand and use. These pre- and post-test assessments allow the teacher to gain knowledge about how well students are performing and allow teachers to construct lesson plans that specifically address gaining the assessed skills.

In most states, accountability assessment does not occur at each grade level. Across the United States these assessments are commonly given at 4th, 8th, and 10th grade. Because of this, districts need to develop pre/post assessments to insure that prerequisite skills are mastered in the grade levels prior to state accountability assessments.

Moreover, it is essential that for every objective taught there are pre/post measures prepared by the district. This will serve a diagnostic purpose as well as provide for mastery of the curriculum objectives. We need to know what students know *before* we begin to teach them (pretest); and we need to know what the students know *after* we have presumably taught them (post-test). If it's important enough to teach, it's important enough to evaluate.

Strategy 10: HOW

1. Identify state accountability benchmark assessments and other external assessments. These include not only tests that are currently in use, but also future tests that are in the planning stage. Most states are moving away from standardized, norm-referenced tests to a combination of criterion-referenced tests and open-ended response items.

2. Disaggregate released test items to identify areas for content and context alignment. Identify the vocabulary, knowledge, and skills assessed. This is an activity that should be teacher in-service session. It provides teachers with a greater understanding of exactly what skills and knowledge students need to be successful on state tests. Do this in conjunction with Strategy 3.

3. Backload developmental skills into earlier grade levels to identify where mastery should take place. All tests assess cumulative knowledge. The level where a skill is tested is not necessarily the level where that skill is mastered. By disaggregating test items and determining where mastery of sub skills takes place, teachers are better able to understand which skills students need at each grade level. Do this in conjunction with Strategy 4.

HOW DO WE ASSESS STUDENT LEARNING?

4. Construct pre/post tests to assess student mastery of necessary vocabulary, knowledge, and skills. If the state test is the first time a student encounters a particular test item format, the student is not likely to perform as well as if she/he had experienced practice with the format during regular instruction.

5. Utilize assessment data to teach and reteach until mastery is achieved.

6. Teachers must teach to mastery and be able to determine when mastery has been achieved. Merely "covering" the material is not sufficient (see also Strategy 28).

7. Develop data entry and tracking systems for students, classes, grades, and schools. This will undoubtedly require the utilization of computer management systems to enable the teacher to continuously update student achievement data. Many such systems are currently available.

8. Treat this sequence as the formative assessment portion of both the curriculum design and its delivery. (For example, classroom instruction and teacher-made tests should be considered part of the formative assessment system.) This system enables teachers to provide extensions, remediation, and enrichment. As the saying goes, "All students do not learn in the same way on the same day." The era when it was acceptable for teachers to feel satisfied if they merely taught the material is over. It is no longer acceptable for teachers to blame society, the economy, the student, or parents for lack of student achievement. While all of

these areas impact student achievement, they do not relieve the teacher from accountability for student achievement.

Strategy 11

Have a Pool of Unsecured Test Item for each Objective

The district provides multiple equivalent (unsecured) criterion-referenced assessments for each objective. These are provided to teachers for use in diagnosing prerequisite skills, acquisition, and mastery of the objectives.

Strategy 11: WHAT

In order for teachers to use ongoing assessments for diagnostic, acquisition, and mastery purposes throughout the instructional process, they need access to a pool of unsecured test items for each curricular objective. This is traditionally accomplished by deconstructing released test items from various external assessments, assessing and identifying the objectives, and backloading them into all grade levels and appropriate content areas. These should be readily available to teachers.

These test items should be easily available to all teachers on computers in their classrooms. Further, teachers should be able to access multiple items simply by placing a request into the system by objective. Such a system can be developed at the district level, or secured from a private vendor.

Teachers are always interested in how well students are doing in acquiring needed skills. However, their time is limited and should be spent primarily in designing individualized instruction, rather than in test item development. Students, too, need to be trained to seek feedback about how well they are doing. Easy access to test items can enable students to prepare their own pre-assessment, before requesting competency assessment from the teacher.

Good assessment is good instruction. The two should not be seen as separate activities. Rather, assessment should reinforce teaching and be considered part of instruction.

In far too many classrooms assessment is not considered instruction. When teachers and students become adept at utilizing the pool of backloaded assessment items matched to the district curriculum, improved achievement is almost assured

This process facilitates the utilization of on-demand assessment by students. That is, when a student feels she/he has achieved the skills to be assessed, she/he requests a post-test from the teacher and takes it. These tests are usually given in class while students are working on a variety of activities. There is little test anxiety because the student is not asked to take the assessment prior to determining that she/he is ready to display the skills necessary.

Strategy 11: WHY

Most of our problems related to improving student achievement are not so much due to the inability of students to learn as they are related to providing an instructional environment where there is a tight relationship among the written, taught, and tested curriculum-in other words, where there is alignment.

The more familiar students are with the content and context of the assessment, the greater the parallelism or transfer of the learning. For example, if the state accountability assessment at the 4th grade level requires a student to write a paragraph with a beginning, middle, and end, a student who has practiced writing many paragraphs with a beginning, middle and end will achieve much more than a student who has only practiced writing topic sentences or completing workbook sheets on grammar.

Access to a pool of unsecured test items serves to inform teachers about what is tested and what form the test will take. This availability also serves to inform students and enable them to take more responsibility for their own learning.

Most important is that the teacher be able to differentiate the teaching of the objectives at the right level of difficulty for each student. Without ongoing assessments, most teachers teach all students in the class the same objective, regardless of whether they have the prerequisites or whether they already know the objective and can demonstrate it in multiple assessment scenarios.

Strategy 11: HOW

1. Obtain lists of district curriculum objectives assessed by content area and grade level.

2. Identify sources of test items in the same format as the state, national, and international accountability assessments. Many companies advertise the availability of parallel test items for almost every state assessment. Buyers beware! First, note any constraints by the state regarding the access of such items. And second, if the district is considering buying such materials, they should be analyzed carefully to make sure there is content and context alignment. It is important to understand that sometimes these items are overused to "drill and kill" student interest and motivation. In this scenario, students may become proficient at doing similar problems without gaining any understanding of the skills necessary for dealing with more difficult problems. While these materials can be useful, they should not be the only source of skill application for students.

3. Conduct a cost-benefit analysis. Is it more costly to buy test items or would it be better to commission curriculum developers or teachers within the district to develop the alternate test items? The development of these alternate test items can be a useful staff development activity.

4. Pilot the test items.

Strategy 12

Establish Secured Performance Benchmark Assessments

The district has secured performance benchmark tests that assess some of the Objectives for each grade level/course. These are administered as pre/post tests at the beginning and near the end of the school year.

Strategy 12: WHAT

Just as there is a need for formative assessment measures to determine how effective teacher instruction has been, there is also a need for periodic, benchmark assessment of a summative nature. Summative evaluation enables educators to know whether they have met their target. The target depicted in *Figure 10* is a symbolic representation of the vocabulary, knowledge and skills assessed on the state accountability measure.

Summative Evaluation: To hit our target, all students must show mastery of state accountability standards.

Figure 10

It is recommended that districts develop summative assessment measures that parallel the state's accountability assessment as well as the district curriculum objectives. These assessments supplement the more frequently given pre/post test assessments developed by teachers.

Summative assessments are referred to as performance benchmark tests. These tests are secured and administered following the same procedures used to administer the state assessments and are common across the school district. While the pre/post test assessments may be included as part of a testing bank available to all teachers in the system, the performance benchmark tests are not.

If the district is large enough and has the expertise necessary to develop reliable and valid parallel assessments, these performance benchmark tests can be constructed internally within the system. However, if the district is small and lacks this area of specialization, it will be necessary to secure these assessments from an outside source. Currently there are many companies offering test construction services.

Strategy 12: WHY

By constructing this internal system of assessment, the district can be assured that all teachers are focusing instruction on the curriculum assessed by the state and expected by the district.

Presently most classroom teachers utilize the textbook as their major resource for instructional planning. This practice is ineffective in producing the type of content and context alignment required. Without district performance assessment there is insufficient assurance of coordination across grades and schools as well as articulation from one level of the system to the next (e.g., elementary to middle school to high school).

Results from benchmark assessment measures enable teachers and administrators to determine to what extent students are achieving across the system, school by school, class by class. With this information, educators can take the necessary steps to refocus instruction on areas of deficiency.

Strategy 12: HOW

1. Treat performance benchmark assessments as summative assessments. A summative assessment is used to determine whether we have met our standard of student achievement or not. It is a periodic line in the sand to determine how well we are doing as a school or a system in achieving stated benchmarks for students. These summative assessments are generally not presented at each grade level. Rather, they measure multiyear achievement in basic skill development. Most typically these assessments are given in the areas of mathematics, reading, and writing; however, the district eventually needs to design them for all subject areas except elective courses.

2. Be sure goals and objectives assessed are understood by the faculty. This mandate should apply to all teachers in all grades and all content areas. The physical education teachers should be as aware of the writing assessment as the art teacher or the reading teacher. Since it is typical for the school to be the unit of accountability today, all teachers in the school are based on the scores of students in the school on very narrow areas of the curriculum. All teachers must accept accountability for all areas of content assessment.

3. Classroom instruction/assessment should "mirror" content/context performance benchmark tests. State testing should not be a time when teachers stop doing what they normally do in classrooms to provide different instruction for test taking. Whatever format is used for the test should sometimes be incorporated into regular classroom instruction through practice exercises and in the classroom testing situations.

4. Arrange for timely scoring. It is not uncommon for results of state assessment measures given in the spring to arrive back in the district in August. States are working hard to shorten this time frame so that teachers have access to the data before school is out. This access enables teachers to analyze these results and determine how they need to modify and adjust their instructional strategies to increase the achievement level of their students. Unfortunately, this is not always possible. School and district leadership should apply whatever pressure it can to

ensure that results are returned to the school in a timely manner, and certainly the district measures should be returned in a timely manner.

5. Identify a school contact person. Each school needs to have an official assessment contact person so that parents, students, and faculty can get a quick response to questions regarding assessment. Most districts have one central office person with this designation. Since assessment accountability has become so important to public education, it is time to provide such a contact.

6. Report results to teachers at all grades, not just the grades tested (see also Strategy 38). Teachers in grade levels not assessed are equally in need of the results so that they can be sure that students at their grade level have achieved mastery of the sub skills necessary for subsequent learning.

7. Ensure that teachers in all content areas are preparing students to achieve at high levels on these tests. If reading scores are low, all teachers in all content areas can be held accountable for providing students with opportunities to read, comprehend, and think critically about what they are learning. These are fundamental skills and not reserved solely for reading class. The art teacher is just as responsible for reading reinforcement as the language arts teacher and should be held accountable for student skill development in this vital area.

8. Link school improvement plans to improved student achievement (see also Strategy 40). Far too often school improvement plans address enabling activities as opposed to student achievement activities. For instance, it is common to see school improvement plans that call for the development of new programs such as after-school childcare. Too often the initiation of these programs becomes an end in itself, and they may not be linked to improved student achievement. Supplementary programs not linked to improved student achievement should be dropped.

9. Require that data from these benchmark assessments be utilized in the school improvement process. This means that specific student results will be reflected in the school improvement plans and targets for improvement will be set. Meeting these requirements is linked to the development or continuation of school site programs. There is an expectation that schools will improve each year (see also Strategy 40).

Strategy 13

Conduct Assessment Training

The district provides adequate training in classroom use of
aligned assessments for directing classroom teaching.

Strategy 13: WHAT

Teachers and building administrators need to be trained in the proper and ethical use of assessments. Many teachers employed in schools today were trained at a time when there were no state accountability systems in place. Norm-referenced tests were commonly used as a sorting mechanism, and teachers rarely saw test results unless they specifically asked for them. There was a general belief that teachers knew best what students should learn and accomplish, and test results were rarely used to make a determination as to whether schools were effective. All of that has changed with the accountability movement.

What we have learned, rather painfully, is not that teachers are doing a poor job in the classroom, but rather, that there has been little focus and connectivity within school systems regarding what students should know and be able to do.

Since attitudes about assessment are firmly linked to a teacher's fundamental belief system, it is of critical importance to provide teachers with the necessary assessment training to ensure that they understand accountability assessment, adopt the dispositions necessary to support accountability assessment, and change their instructional planning to assure congruence among the written, taught, and tested curriculum.

Strategy 13: WHY

Most classroom teachers today remember when it was necessary to sign a document attesting to adherence to a testing code of ethics. These documents were prepared by state departments of education to ensure that teachers were not testing students using the exact test items that would appear on a state accountability test. To do so was (and still is) considered a breach of ethics that merited severe penalties, sometimes even loss of license.

For some teachers, adhering to a testing code of ethics has been mistakenly interpreted to mean that teaching the skills assessed on the state accountability test is a violation of the code. Fortunately, the number of teachers who presently believe this is small.

What is also unclear to many other teachers is the degree to which it is ethical to teach to the test learnings. This is especially troublesome in states that continue to use a norm-referenced test as their measure of accountability.

The vast majority of states are moving to a state accountability system based on criterion-referenced testing. In these states, the objectives students are to learn are stated, made available to teachers, and form the basis for the development of the state test. These states routinely make sample test items available to teachers so that teachers can develop instruction aligned to the state assessment.

Regardless of the type of state assessment used, all teachers need a clear understanding of the assessments in use. As the district builds the items pool, pre/post tests, and benchmark performance assessments, teachers need to understand the system and how to use it in order to maximize student achievement.

Strategy 13: HOW

Try the following steps:
1. Identify the most commonly used traditional and authentic assessment instruments used to assess student achievement. All teachers in the system must be aware of these assessments and understand how these assessments are used to make accountability decisions within the school. This information should not be confined simply to the content areas assessed, such as mathematics and reading. Rather, all teachers at all grade levels should understand the accountability assessments used within the system; they should also understand that they are accountable for ensuring that students achieve well on these assessments.

2. Focus initial training on types of instruments used for accountability assessment. While initial training should focus on state-mandated accountability assessments, additional training should be provided for all district-wide assessments used within the system.

3. Identify assessment trainers/coaches. Since teachers vary considerably in their knowledge and understanding of assessment, it is worthwhile to appoint school assessment trainers/coaches with the same stipend paid to athletic trainers/coaches.

4. Develop training modules over time for use over time with teachers of varying levels of expertise/competence:
   - Novice-For newly hired teachers
     ✧ Provides overview of accountability instruments. These teachers are generally non-tenured, inexperienced teachers working in their first job. What they know about assessment is usually confined to what they learned in their pre-service training. The reality of accountability assessment is often foreign to them and they need help in understanding how these assessments impact their instructional planning.
   - Professional-For experienced teachers
     ✧ Provides information about a wide variety of traditional and authentic assessments. Professional teachers have usually been in the system for some time. Their skills in the area of assessment can be expanded to include a wider variety of assessments, including more authentic assessment techniques.
     ✧ Trains professional teachers to serve as assessment coaches. Professional teachers often enjoy the role of assessment coach for a novice teacher. By serving in this role, the professional teacher gains additional competence and self-esteem and continues to move toward the role of expert teacher.
   - Expert-For teachers wanting to keep abreast of the latest developments in assessment
     ✧ Provides opportunities for study groups, outside district training and stipends for teaching in-service sessions to district staff. Teachers at this level can serve as the district's cutting-edge experts. They enjoy following the latest research on effective assessment strategies and can be influential in bringing this information back to the district.

5. Develop examples of quality anchor assessments suitable for use at a variety of grade levels and content areas. Anchor assessments enable teachers to see actual examples of quality work at each grade level. These assessments can also be used as examples of exemplary work and shared with students.

6. Train staff in the utilization of the assessment technology programs. A large number of companies are developing assessment technology programs to enable teachers to construct individualized tests for students. All districts should be investigating these programs and investing in appropriate technology and software so those teachers can construct on-demand tests for students.

7. Provide focus group opportunities for teachers to talk about their attitudes regarding the utilization of assessment items. With the large proportion of teachers who still have negative feelings about teaching to tests, these focus groups offer an opportunity for them to through their opposition to assessment.

8. Create a professional assessment library. Every school should have a large inventory of professional development materials in the area of assessment. These can include videotapes, books, journal articles, and research studies.

Strategy 14

Use Assessments Diagnostically

Teachers use the assessments to gain diagnostic data on student learning of the objectives (prerequisite skills acquisition and mastery), to assess the program assessment, and to direct instruction.

Strategy 14: WHAT

Using assessments diagnostically should take place at both the school and classroom levels in addition to the district level. These assessment data should be disaggregated by gender, ethnicity, and socioeconomic level (see also Strategies 17 and 38). Trend analyses should be developed to track patterns over time.

At the building level, school principals should routinely analyze test data to determine current, overall levels of student achievement and to project realistic, yearly goals. These data should become the basic needs assessment for school improvement plans, and should be shared with interested stakeholders in the community via newsletters, press releases, and presentations. It should be understood that the school and staff operate from a data-driven culture. When new programs are designed, they should be databased with a clear link between program objectives and improved student achievement (see also Strategy 19).

Classroom teachers should review assessment data to determine where students are achieving and where additional instruction is needed. Teachers should be able to identify subgroups in the classroom that need extra support and provide for that support in the regular classroom. If outside support is offered, there should be clear communication between the classroom teacher and the support teacher in order to maximize improved results.

Both building principals and classroom teachers should practice the concept of deep alignment. Figure 11 is a depiction of the concept.

Figure 11

The Nature of the Reconnect with Deep Alignment

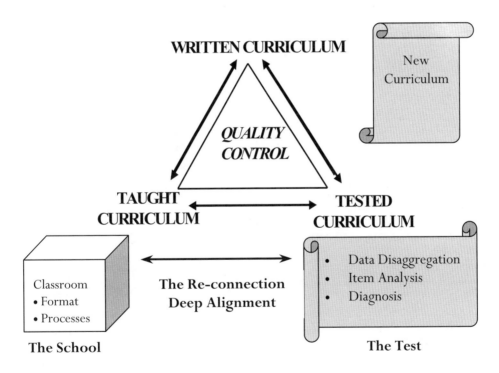

This figure represents the nature of how teachers need to use test data to design new instructional practices for students who have not mastered the skills assessed. First, when new curriculum is introduced, it is assumed that the concept of quality control is in place; that is, there is a relationship among the written, taught, and tested curriculum. When a test is initially given to determine whether students have achieved the skills, data is disaggregated by a variety of criteria such as socioeconomic class, gender and ethnicity.

Then the classroom teacher designs new instruction, termed here as the *reconnect*, so that more students are mastering the skills. The tests to be disaggregated may be at any level, and may be classroom pre/post tests, benchmark performance tests, or state accountability assessments.

Strategy 14: WHY

The volume of things to teach is limitless but the time to teach them it is finite. Instructional time is probably our most valuable resource; we cannot afford to use it unwisely. By using data disaggregation techniques, teachers and school principals can maximize the use of instructional time.

When a data-driven culture is created in classrooms and schools, a new synergy arises because teachers and students can see, track, and celebrate their success.

Strategy 14: HOW

1. Ensure that teachers are using the pool of assessment items on a regular basis in the classroom to diagnose where each student is in his/her learning and to use this data to differentiate the instruction (see also Strategy 30).

2. Utilize the "Pareto Principle" (a few account for the many) to determine instructional priorities from the analysis of assessment results. Raising an average score is accomplished by dealing with the largest group of students in a common area (for example, by quartile) and improving their scores. The greater the gain by those nearest the bottom, the more impact there is on raising average scores (greater than by raising the scores of those at the top). This is true if the number of students in the bottom quartile is greater than the number of students near the top, which is typically the case.

3. At the beginning of the school year provide classroom teachers with student achievement results for the new class (based on previous assessments) as well as those for last year's class. This enables the teacher to understand the skill deficiencies of the present class and also determine deficiencies experienced the year prior. Conduct an item-by-item analysis of class results. This item analysis enables teachers to understand the specific areas of skill deficiency both of students entering the class at the beginning of the year and students who had been in the teacher's class last year.

4. Determine skill areas to focus on from the item analysis. More instructional time will need to be devoted to the areas of deficiency for the students entering the class at the beginning of the year. In addition, the teacher will have to develop

alternative instructional strategies for the areas of deficiency of students who had been in the teacher's class the year prior.

5. Develop parallel test items to assess the prerequisite skills that students should have mastered coming into the course. These pretests will help the teacher identify specific skill deficiencies.

6. Identify students requiring development support. Not all students in the class will need additional instruction and time for guided practice, but those who do need this help must be targeted or their future learning will not be successful.

7. Determine type of support needed. By pinpointing the area of difficulty, students can be provided with focused instruction and coaching to overcome the deficiency.

8. Current instructional materials must be reviewed to determine if they provide for content and context alignment. If not, additional support materials will need to be acquired or developed by the teacher.

9. Make needed adjustments to maximize alignment.

10. Develop "deeply aligned" test items. Deeply aligned test items not only ask the student to apply skills assessed on parallel test items, they require that test items demand more sophisticated transfer. For instance, if an item calls for interpretation of a single bar graph, a deeply aligned item may require interpretation of a multibar graph.

Strategy 15

Teach Students to Be "Test Wise"

Teachers teach students test-taking skills that are aligned to the type of high-stakes tests being administered at the national, state, and district levels.

Strategy 15: WHAT

To be "test wise" is to understand how tests are formatted and how to properly record answers. Without this knowledge, students do not perform as well as they could. They know the information but lack knowledge of the testing approach. Students should not fear the testing situation. Fear usually comes from the unknown. When students learn about the nature of tests, practice successfully completing them, and think about how they accomplished what they did, the fear of the testing situation is dissipated.

Strategy 15: WHY

Once again, this is the doctrine of "no surprises." By preparing students to anticipate what may be on the test and providing them with the skills necessary to approach the testing situation, students are empowered. These students tend not to be hampered with test phobia. They know they have been successful in parallel testing situations, so they go into a new testing situation confident that they will be successful. When students are test wise, it is their knowledge that is tested, rather than their ability to take a particular type of test.

Strategy 15: HOW

1. Practice the doctrine of "no surprises." Be sure that students have had ample opportunity to practice both the content and context of the various assessments they may encounter.

2. Utilize accountability test context during regular, ongoing instruction. Accountability assessment can take many forms including multiple-choice items, true/false, matching, completion, open-ended response items, interpretative essays, and others. Teachers should be familiar with the format of the accountability testing and use this format often in class as part of practice activities and/or classroom assessments.

3. Develop test-taking rubrics and teach them to students. Students like to use scoring rubrics. Test-taking rubrics enable students to have a predetermined method for approaching a problem. For example, a test-taking rubric for responding to a multiple choice test item might include the following:
   - Look for vague words such as "some" or "often." These are typically used in correct responses.
   - Watch for long and precisely stated responses. These are often the correct ones.
   - If the words used do not make sense or do not read smoothly with the stem, the response is probably not correct.
   - Choices with grammatical or spelling errors are probably not correct.

4. Have students engage in self-assessment and peer assessment using the rubrics. No student should read a question without having some idea of how to respond. If there is an open-ended response item on a test, such as one that asks students to

identify the advantages and disadvantages of some course of action, there should have been many opportunities for students to encounter parallel items during part of the regular classroom instruction.

5. Construct metacognition lessons dealing with test-taking strategies. Teach lessons where students describe how they would respond to common types of questions, e.g., predict an outcome, cause and effect, or take a position and defend it. Have students discuss how they approach these responses and provide suggestions for how they should proceed.

6. Provide good instructions for the testing situation. If students do not understand the test directions, the chances are the results will not be good.

7. Review key concepts and objectives that will appear on the test; do this periodically throughout the year and again prior to the accountability assessment. The type of review enables students to revisit material previously mastered, provides an opportunity for students to practice, and enables them to ask questions to clarify any points that are not well understood.

Strategy 16

Establish a Reasonable Testing
Schedule and Environment

*The district staff and school staff provide a reasonable schedule of testing
as well as a proper physical setting for all assessment situations.*

Strategy 16: WHAT

Every effort should be made to ensure that students and staff are as comfortable as possible with the testing schedule and environment. The testing schedule should be planned far in advance and incorporated into the district's yearly calendar. Every effort should be made to avoid conflicts. Scheduling assessments the week before or after a vacation is not a good idea. The week before breaks is often filled with activity related to what will happen on the break. Also, students and staff need some time after a vacation to become reoriented to the school routine and to refocus their attention.

The testing environment should parallel the teaching environment as much as possible. Tests should be administered in the class where instruction takes place, if at all possible. Students generally do better if they take the mathematics assessment in the room where they have their math class, and with their math teacher present. This environment enables students to better visualize solutions to problems. It also helps reduce the anxiety commonly associated with the testing situation. If the ideas we suggest have been put into place, chances are that the students will feel fairly comfortable.

If possible, students should be able to have outlets for their anxiety. The addition of squeezable rubber balls or other kinesthetic stress relievers, munchies, and access to water are all factors designed to reduce stress.

If students have been properly prepared for the test, this should be an opportunity for them to show what they can do, and they should be encouraged to approach the task with that point of view.

Strategy 16: WHY

It should be remembered that any assessment only measures a small part of the taught curriculum. As depicted in *Figure 12,* the definition of test achievement is measured learning.

Figure 12

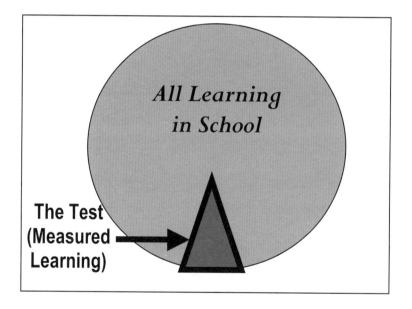

In this example, the circle represents all the learning in school, the square represents concepts presented via the test, and the triangle represents test achievement, or the learning that is measured by the test. As you can see, much of what is tested in this example is not taught in school. How did the students do on such a test? Chances are, not too well.

The small area at the right hand corner of the testing square represents the limited congruence between what is taught in school and what is assessed.

Figure 13 shows an example of no alignment, surface alignment, and what we like to call "deep test alignment." To achieve deep test alignment, what is assessed is completely embedded in the taught curriculum.

Figure 13

QUALITY CONTROL

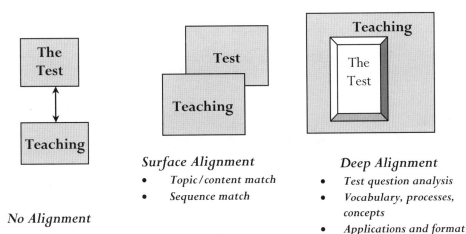

No Alignment

Surface Alignment
- *Topic/content match*
- *Sequence match*

Deep Alignment
- *Test question analysis*
- *Vocabulary, processes, concepts*
- *Applications and format match*
- *Student practice in class*

Strategy 16: HOW

1. Match the testing schedule to what we know about student attention span. The attention span of the elementary child can range from 15 to 30 minutes. Placing students in testing situations where they have to remain focused for several hours at a time is not conducive to producing the best results.
2. Assess in regular classrooms. Familiar surroundings enable the students to relax.
3. Provide for various learning modalities. If possible the testing situation should accommodate for students that need to get up and move around for short periods of time as well as for students who work best in private areas such as learning carrels. It should be acceptable for a variety of different testing situations to be accommodated in the same classroom.
4. Make sure parents are aware of the testing schedule. Parents should be encouraged to talk with their children about the importance of the tests. Parents should be made aware of the format of the tests and should be encouraged to help their children become familiar with this format.

Strategy 17

Disaggregate Assessment Data

District assessments, as well as external assessments, are disaggregated by student, teacher, course/class/grade level, gender, race, socioeconomic level, and primary language and are used in making program and classroom decisions.

Strategy 17: WHAT

Data disaggregation refers to "taking apart" tests results to a level of specificity to enable central office administrators, principals, and classroom teachers to see what skills are being assessed and what to do to improve test results. This practice is essential for improving student achievement results. The level of disaggregation should enable professionals within the system to make decisions regarding what to teach and reteach, what materials to use, and what teaching strategies to employ.

Data disaggregation should bring the level of analysis to the classroom. With these data teachers should be able to determine which students have mastered specific skills. The disaggregation should include analysis by student, teacher, course/class/grade level, gender race, socioeconomic level and primary language where appropriate.

In order to disaggregate achievement results, it is necessary that the district/school have a written curriculum that is clearly aligned to the assessment system in regard to content and context alignment. Such a written curriculum will enable staff to determine where the breakdown in student mastery has occurred. It may be at the grade level where the test is administered or it may be at preceding grade levels.

Strategy 17: WHY

Without accurate, current disaggregated data, administrators and classroom teachers do not have enough information to focus and connect their work and ultimately improve student achievement.

State departments of education are increasing accountability practices by passing legislation that mandates district and school accountability for "all children learning at high levels." Currently, most of this legislation is directed toward documenting student achievement in the areas of mathematics, reading and writing, but more and more states are expanding the areas of accountability to include science and social studies. Some states, such as Kentucky, assess the areas of fine arts and vocational education.

State departments of education are also expanding the types of assessment they are mandating. While some states, (Georgia, California, and Idaho) may still use a standardized, norm-referenced test to determine school accountability, other states, (Virginia and Indiana) use criterion-referenced tests. Kentucky still uses open-ended response items (short essays) in addition to other types of assessment. Most states are continually upgrading the tests and often making them more difficult. Texas and Florida are examples of states actively engaged in using the state assessment system as a mechanism for increasing expectations of what students should know and be able to do.

No school or district administration can afford to ignore state accountability measures. Even schools with traditionally high achievement levels must now be concerned with the achievement levels of all subgroups within the system. In the past, schools serving large percentages of students from high socioeconomic levels were content to report average achievement data for all students. Many states are now requiring that achievement data be reported by gender, ethnicity, and socioeconomic class (percentage of students on free and reduced lunch). This reporting mechanism makes visible the discrepancy between these groups and highlights the fact that, generally, students qualifying for free and reduced lunch, African-American males, and students of Hispanic origin score lower on state-mandated tests than other students.

Granted, the American system of public education has not met the needs of all of the children of all of the people. Now that high test scores have become the political agenda of almost every governor and many legislators across the country. Given the public visibility of the student achievement data, this has lead to the proliferation of high-stakes legislation that has placed significantly higher demands on public school educators.

The student ultimately pays the price for failing to achieve these expectations. Students are placed, labeled, and sorted by the scores they achieve on these assessments. It is becoming more popular to label administrators and teachers based on these scores. All of this requires that everyone in the system, including the students and parents, understand the concept of alignment, how it impacts student achievement, and what that means for improving the accountability measures of the system.

All of this applies equally well to the district's assessment system. If a district has a unified assessment system, data must be disaggregated by the same categories: gender, ethnicity, and socioeconomic level. As a caveat, systems claim they are "better" than the results of the state accountability system would indicate. The general public does not understand that this idea is sometimes true. It could be true that the district assessment system assesses much higher order skills than the state assessment system. If so, the district needs to report the results of these assessments in the same way that the state requires. Even with that, the public has difficulty accepting that the notion that students can perform poorly on state-mandated tests and still be learning at high levels.

Professional educators can no longer ignore district and school results on mandated tests. Moreover, and perhaps even more importantly, the mission of the district should always be to increase student achievement. It is our business. It is what we are all about-producing learning!

Strategy 17: HOW

The following steps are recommended for student achievement data disaggregation.

1. The improvement of student achievement becomes one of the central goals of the organization and is included as a measure of performance for teachers, school administrators, and central office staff.
2. All teachers and administrators within the system accept their responsibility to be held accountable for improving student achievement.
3. When the district receives achievement data, it is synthesized by student, teacher, and school and reported to school administrators.
4. These data include an item analysis by student and class configuration so that a given teacher can analyze these data by the current and preceding class.
5. Teachers are expected to be able to interpret these data and relate them to instructional planning.
6. Teachers are expected to design instructional strategies to remediate deficiencies that lead to student mastery of essential skills.
7. All educators in the system are expected to understand the concepts of content and context alignment.

8. Teachers are expected to analyze present instructional materials and determine the content and context alignment with the assessment system.
9. Teachers are expected to modify, expand, and adjust the present instructional materials to bring them in better alignment with the assessments.
10. Written curriculum documents should be aligned with the state and district assessment systems.
11. Building administrators are expected to monitor the implementation of the district curriculum.
12. The district is expected to have developed a formative student achievement assessment system that will enable teachers to receive data regarding student mastery, all in sufficient time to remediate deficiencies so that students will achieve mastery before the summative evaluation.
13. District personnel should provide parents and the public with appropriate information regarding the concept of alignment and what it means for student achievement.
14. Parent groups need to work actively within the system to mentor parents who traditionally do not support the schools in order to assure that there is positive parental support for students doing well on the state and district assessments.
15. Provide the board with periodic updates regarding strategies to improve student achievement.
16. Include in these reports the trend data over time for all of the subgroups within the system.
17. Continue to hold everyone in the system accountable for sustaining improvement of student achievement over time.

Strategy 18
Maintain Student Progress Reports

Teachers maintain individual student progress reports by district objectives; students and parents are knowledgeable about the student's progress on such objectives.

Strategy 18: WHAT

Reporting student progress is both a formative and summative event. Typically, the reporting mechanism used today consists of quarterly report cards with letter grades at the intermediate and secondary level and with either letter grades at the secondary level and above or some variation of "satisfactory," "unsatisfactory," and "outstanding" at the primary level. At the intermediate and secondary levels there is often no consistent definition for the meaning of letter grades across content area, teachers, grades, or schools. Two teachers may teach Algebra I in the same high school and both teachers usually maintain their own grading system. Consequently a "B" in one class may or may not denote the same level of learning as a "B" in another class.

What we mean by reporting student progress refers to the mechanism a school or district has in place to provide students, teachers, parents, and district administrators with clear, consistent feedback about how well students are achieving the mastery level skills, content, and knowledge included in the district's core curriculum. Again, it should be noted that the skills designated in the district core curriculum are those that students must be able to demonstrate at mastery level. This means that the mastery level has been defined in specific enough terms to enable a teacher to make a judgment about whether one student has achieved the objectives and another has not. This requires a totally different level of specificity from the one currently in use with our present grading system.

This type of reporting system requires that teachers have access to a pool of assessments that can be used throughout the year to determine student mastery. Some districts have purchased test management systems that enable teachers to identify objectives to be assessed, and then a computer program constructs the test. Other districts or schools have trained teachers to construct assessments. While there is no one way that is considered best, it is necessary to provide some kind of assistance to teachers so that these assessments are available.

Strategy 18: WHY

In order for students, teachers, and parents to understand that student achievement on district and state tests is important, everyone must understand why these tests are given and the value of receiving information about how well students are performing. If the stance of the district is that these assessments are not important, teachers and students are more likely not to take them too seriously. By making clear to everyone that these assessments are regarded as a serious accountability measure for the system, and by providing the necessary information to inform everyone about how well individual students, schools, and the district are doing, it is possible to change the attitude of those receiving information about these assessments.

HOW DO I TEACH SO *EACH* STUDENT LEARNS?

For example, everyone who takes driver's training knows that the training is designed to enable the participant to successfully drive a car, have knowledge of the state statutes regarding motor vehicle safety, and display that knowledge and skill by passing a multiple-choice test and driver's test. Successfully driving the car is a performance event designed to ensure that the candidate not only has content knowledge but can apply that knowledge in a real-world setting. Mastery level expectations are clearly specified. The format of the performance event and the multiple-choice test are known. There seems to be no difficulty in maintaining student motivation or in explaining to parents why these courses are offered. Even the use of driving simulators is not questioned-it is understood that they are used to assist students in understanding their skill level and helping them improve.

Providing students with formative and summative feedback is common practice in most of our vocational education courses, fine and performing arts, physical education courses and, more recently, technology applications. Understanding the relationship between formative feedback and how it relates to summative assessment is not a concept foreign to educators. The relationship between formative assessment on mandated district and state accountability assessments needs to be made clearer so that it is well understood by everyone in the system.

Strategy 18: HOW

1. Identify all district-and state-mandated assessments.
2. Review the content and context of each assessment.
3. Develop a testing schedule and distribute to teachers, parents, and administrators.
4. Develop a plan to provide teachers and students with formative assessment information at timely intervals throughout the year prior to the summative assessment point. These procedures should include information of a formative nature for grade level teachers instructing in those grades prior to the assessment grade. For instance, if the state assessments are given in 4th, 8th and 11th grade, the formative measures should provide teachers instructing in kindergarten through 3rd grade with information about student mastery of the enabling skills students must have in order to demonstrate mastery on the summative test given in 4th grade.
5. Select or develop additional assessments for those skill and content areas not assessed as part of the state system.
6. Supplement or modify the current grading system and report cards to provide students and parents with information about student mastery of core curriculum competencies.
7. Provide the necessary information to parents and students to enable them to understand why these assessments are given and how information about student mastery will be provided.
8. Design procedures for both a formative and summative evaluation of the system to provide student progress reports.

❧ Analysis of Standard Two ❧

Now it is time for you to evaluate the status of your school or school district on *Standard Two: Provide Assessments Aligned to the Curriculum*. For each strategy think about what the current status of your situation is regarding these strategies and the changes you feel are needed. Write your responses in the spaces provided.

STRATEGY	CURRENT STATUS	CHANGES NEEDED
10. Develop Aligned District Pre/Post Criterion-Referenced Assessments	❑Adequate ❑Not adequate	
11. Have a Pool of Unsecured Test Items for each Objective	❑Adequate ❑Not adequate	
12. Establish Secured Performance Benchmark Assessments	❑Adequate ❑Not adequate	
13. Conduct Assessment Training	❑Adequate ❑Not adequate	
14. Use Assessments Diagnostically	❑Adequate ❑Not adequate	
15. Teach Students to Be "Test Wise"	❑Adequate ❑Not adequate	
16. Establish a Reasonable Testing Schedule and Environment	❑Adequate ❑Not adequate	
17. Disaggregate Assessment Data	❑Adequate ❑Not adequate	
18. Maintain Student Progress Reports	❑Adequate ❑Not adequate	

STANDARD THREE

Align Program and Instructional Resources to the Curriculum and Provide Student Equality and Equity

The following are nine highly powerful strategies regarding programs, resources, and student equity that can be used to attain higher student achievement:

19. *Align Programs to the Curriculum to Ensure Congruity*

20. *Use Research and Data that Document Results to Drive Program Selection, and Validate the Implementation of Programs with Action Research*

21. *Evaluate Programs to Determine Effectiveness to Strengthen Student Achievement of Curriculum Objectives*

22. *Ensure that Textbooks and Instructional Resources Are Aligned to the District Curriculum Objectives and Assessments in Both Content and Context Dimensions*

23. *Use Technology in Design or Selection Procedures to Ensure Strong Connections to System Learning Expectations and Feedback*

24. *Provide Training in the Use of Instructional Resources and Their Alignment with System Curriculum Objectives-Content, Context, and Cognitive Level*

25. *Select or Modify Instructional Resources for Lessons to Ensure Full Alignment with System Objectives and Tested Learning*

26. *Place Students in Programs and Activities in an Equitable Manner and with Equal Access to the Curriculum*

27. *Implement Effective Programs and Strategies with English Language Learners*

Strategy 19

Align Programs to the Curriculum to Ensure Congruity

All formal and informal programs are investigated for their alignment to the district curriculum objectives and modifications are made to ensure high alignment.

Strategy 19: WHAT

Programs used in schools need to be checked for alignment to system objectives and affirmed, modified, or terminated to assure consequential congruity. This strategy ensures that the school system is reducing fragmentation, contradiction, and rudderless activity within the organization. Sound curriculum management takes steps to eliminate activities that are unrelated, irrelevant, or unnecessary in terms of accomplishing the system's defined learner objectives. Given little or no congruity of programs with the system's learning objectives, the system will be less than effective in accomplishing its purposes.

Once the system defines what it expects students to learn (know, think, do, feel, or be like), it is essential that the system take specific steps to secure programs and to deliver services designed to accomplish the system's expectations. Unfortunately, program or strategic choices are often less focused on an organization's purposes than on its ways of doing things. For example, many programs address specific teaching skills but overlook what content is taught or in which context it is taught. Good teaching helps, of course, but good teaching has to teach *something relevant* to the expectations or the assessment criterion in place.

Curriculum management requires the principal or educational administrator to connect program activities, teaching strategies, and formal or informal organizational conduct with what learners are expected to learn. This connection and the flow of activity is illustrated in *Figure 14* below.

Figure 14

Connectivity of Programs and System Objectives

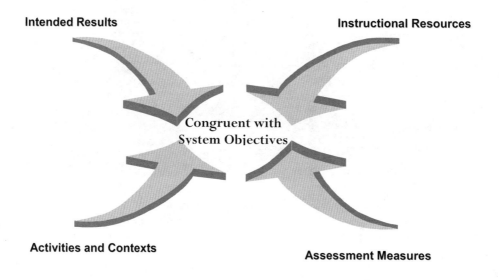

What do the elements in *Figure 14* indicate? Each element is important in assuring quality control in achieving the aims and purposes of the school system as interpreted by the assessment framework.

A well-connected curriculum demonstrates high levels of congruity between the intended results of programs selected for use in the system and the intended results of the system, most often system objectives. Any program selected for use in a school system will have factors and attributes that characterize its intended outcomes or effects. Programs also may be measured for the level of instructional efficacy they have demonstrated in actual use and application. The intended outcomes and expectations of any program must be carefully considered and examined against the system objectives. If there is a good fit between what the program intends to deliver and what the system wants, then the program may be worth implementing on a trial basis.

Instructional resources, including the use of time available for instruction, must also demonstrate cohesion with the systems learner objectives of the system. Time available for teaching and learning is precious, and it must be carefully budgeted. If time is wasted or inefficiently used, the system's ability to achieve its purposes may be sub-optimized or undermined. (For other resource alignment issues, see Strategy 22.)

Activities and contexts must match or align with system objectives for learners. The connection students make between assessment item contexts and classroom contexts must be unconstrained and clearly evident. If a concept is measured by the assessment in a certain context, students without prior experience in that context (i.e., word problems in math, inquiry-type questions requiring inductive thinking in science, etc.) will be disadvantaged and performance success will be diminished.

Assessment measures employed on a day-to-day basis must also reflect the intended learner outcomes or achievement expectations implied by the system's mission and statement of objectives. For example, if a program is evaluated on the basis of student, parent, or teacher perceptions, but the system objectives specify a particular cognitive skill result, the evaluation may be positive and encouraging regardless of actual performance or results in achievement of the intended skill.

The competent curriculum manager needs to check and verify that program intentions, resources used, types of activities selected, and assessment measures utilized at the classroom level align and demonstrate high congruency with the system's defined objectives and assessment modes.

Strategy 19: WHY

Attainment of a specific goal is not unlike climbing a mountain. Choosing a route that leads elsewhere will subvert accomplishment. Spending too much time thinking and planning about the route will subvert accomplishment. Picking equipment that breaks down and fails halfway up the mountain will subvert accomplishment. Hopping on one foot, even though it is helpful to physical conditioning, may subvert reaching the peak as well. It is easy to see how many activities, sometimes even those that are fun to do, can get in the way of attaining an objective. This often holds true for schools.

For decades, what teachers were to do in the classrooms or the selection of programs for use in a given school depended upon the vicissitudes of individual or school choices. Such choices were often based upon the popularity of some programs (due to the vagaries of trends) or on the intrinsic nature of the activities, rather than upon demonstrated evidence of results relative to assessment. However, with underperforming schools, only those learnings germane to the measure of the assessment system are worth selecting or maintaining within the system. Popular or favorite programs must stand scrutiny against desired results, but often such connections are not made.

Unless strong connections are established that ensure parallelism between program content, contexts, resource use, and demonstrated results and system objectives, the school has little or no control over its fate or achievement. Investigating and verifying that program characteristics and features are consonant with system ends helps surmount one of the key factors often undermining achievement–the fragmentation and inconsistency of organizational effort. Building consistency and harmony between deeds and intended results will maximize achievement performance.

Strategy 19: HOW

The following steps are suggested to implement this strategy:

1. Conduct an inventory of all programs currently implemented within a school or school system. List each program by name, identify the nature of its objectives, locate and fix its grade level boundaries, delineate its strategies and methodologies, and determine how each program is measured for success.

2. After deconstruction of the achievement instrument (see Strategy 1), identify system objectives and learner expectations with as much specificity as possible for each grade level.

3. Investigate or check actual program results against system objectives, if possible. For example, locate any specific assessment items that measure the program's intended results, and identify levels of success in terms of student mastery of the expectation.

4. Match program intentions or results with system objectives or desired results, item by item. Map out the matches, overlaps, gaps, and discrepancies between program results or expectations and system objectives. Determine the level of the match in terms of percentage, i.e., the program addresses X percent of the system objectives.

5. If the program effectively addresses 50 percent or more of the system objectives, it is worthy of modification and improvement efforts to increase its efficacy. If the program effectively addresses 70 percent or more of the objectives of the system, it is adequate. Less than a 50 percent match indicates that the program needs to be considered for termination.

6. Require that all future and new program requests or proposals demonstrate a match between system objectives and the program's intentions. In addition, all new programs that appear congruent with system objectives need to be pilot-

tested for actual results within the system. A small-scale implementation with careful monitoring of results (see Strategy 17) should demonstrate at least 70 percent congruence with the system's desired results prior to implementation across the system.

With careful attention to aligning programs with system objectives, the underperforming school can avoid and overcome historical patterns of incongruity between the plethora of programs available to system mission and objectives.

Strategy 20

Use Research and Data that Document Results to Drive Program Selection and Validate the Implementation of Programs with Action Research

Programs selected for use are research and data driven. Further, the school staff members collect their own action research on the programs selected.

Strategy 20: WHAT

Choosing programs is not an easy task. For the school practitioner, it is difficult, often impossible, to know ahead of time whether or not a program proposal is based upon research or is simply a current fad that has gained substantial momentum. Without research, it is safe to say that programs vary in nature and type, and they widely differ in efficacy and results.

Discernment in selecting programs is called for in the effective curriculum leader, and such discernment needs to be based largely upon documented evidence of results and on research validation. There are criteria to employ in discerning whether or not a program is successful or worthwhile, and such criteria require substantiation through careful and systematic research in educational institutions.

Given good foundations of research for program selection, the school curriculum leader can be assured that using research will prevent unsuitable selection of program alternatives. Strategies to assist school administrators in determining program efficacy are available, but in studies conducted by curriculum auditors over the past decade, seldom are rational research findings used in choosing programs for implementation in schools.

Even after adoption and implementation of programs, too seldom does the educational institution conduct its own research to determine if the program is meeting the need it was designated to address. Without empirical evidence, program selection and/or implementation encounters significant risk that results may impair achievement and thwart system accomplishment of its aims and purposes. With empirical evidence, decisions on program selection and implementation are more likely to reflect assurance that results will be in keeping with design.

Strategy 20: WHY

Evidence of program effectiveness ahead of time provides the administrator with greater precision in selecting and implementing programmatic options and alternatives to deliver organizational aims and purposes. Given good information about previous research on a specific program option or alternative, the educational leader can make better decisions relative to choosing, keeping, or dropping programs. Better decisions are characterized as resulting in greater organizational effectiveness, less wasted effort and resources, and greater satisfaction of the learning needs of clientele.

A plethora of program options have been tried in many schools without research justification. For example, consider the following list of program options that was implemented in one large Midwestern school system (*Figure 15*).

Figure 15

Elementary Supplemental Programs Operating in
1999 Midwestern School District
(65 Elementary Schools)

1.	AARP Tutors	2.	Accelerated Reader
3.	Adopt-A-School	4.	After School tutoring
5.	AME Zion Reading	6.	America Reads
7.	Attendance Partners	8.	Curriculum Alignment
9.	Direct Reading Instruction	10.	Early Literacy
11.	Early Reading Workshop	12.	East High Mentors
13.	East of High Street tutoring	14.	Expanded Learning Opportunity
15.	Family Focus Centers	16.	Gladden Tutoring

Figure 15 continued

17. Grandparents Tutors	18. HOSTS
19. I Know I Can: Peer Mediation	20. IBM Tutors
21. Mt. Carmel Adapters Tutoring	22. ODE Phonics Grants
23. Ohio Wesleyan Tutors	24. OSU Tutoring
25. Parent Tutors	26. Parent Volunteer Reading
27. Peaceful Schools	28. Peer Counseling
29. Peer Mediation	30. Peer Tutoring
31. Proficiency Intervention	32. Proficiency Saturday Tutoring
33. Proficiency Tutoring	34. Reading/Math After School Tutoring
35. RIF-Reading is Fundamental	36. Rolling Readers
37. Science/Math Workshop	38. SFA-Success for All
39. SMART	40. South High Mentors
41. Sylvan School	42. Target Teach
43. Title I Pullout Reading	44. Title I Math
45. UHC Proficiency Tutoring	46. USI
47. Work Study Tutors	

In this one district alone, 47 different program options were tried in the elementary schools. When staff members were asked for data on the performance or success of these programs, only three of the programs had such information. In this case, the school system is implementing many programmatic options, but the system is not determining if the programs are valid, appropriate, or producing desired results.

The enormity of problems resulting from such haphazard or aimless program selection and implementation compels us to note that, under such circumstances, it is no surprise that most of the schools in the system shown in *Figure 15* are underperforming. The "shotgun" approach fails.

Strategy 20: HOW

Use of research is essential to assure sound decision-making relative to program selection and implementation. To use program research properly, follow the suggested steps below. Effective research includes the following ten steps:

1. Ascertain the current situation within the given school or system (use appropriate assessment information).
2. Identify the problems or needs that are evident and delineate them.
3. Identify options and alternatives (programs or services) that address the problems and needs identified.

4. Develop a formal framework with goals and measurable objectives to address the problems or needs. (What will it take to solve this problem or to meet the need? What will resolution of the issues look like?)
5. Select a program alternative that seems to address the problem or need.
6. Request from the program source (or proposing individual or group) the results produced by this program option.
7. Review the information provided. (Note: If none provided, conduct a search for evidence and/or empirical information about use of this program).
8. Profile research findings against system objectives using the data gathered through the evaluation.
9. Determine the level and efficacy of relevance of the research and documented results; if the evidence indicates a strong result, from the program's implementation, it may be considered for adoption.
10. After implementing the program, continue to conduct research on the program's efficacy in meeting the needs of the organization.

Programs that have not been scrutinized in this process often do not address district needs, priorities, and goals and do not sustain productivity. Implementation of programs is a complex process, which must be carefully managed and based on sound research if desired results are to be realized.

Strategy 21

Evaluate Programs to Determine Effectiveness to Strengthen Student Achievement of Curriculum Objectives

Programs are evaluated to determine effectiveness in achieving student achievement on the curricular objectives.

Strategy 21: WHAT

A successful leader needs to meet two essential requirements for organizational effectiveness. First, the leader must know what the purposes of the organization are—what is the organization trying to accomplish? Second, the leader must be able to determine how well the organization is achieving its purposes. It is the leader's responsibility to clarify and disseminate the organization's purpose, vision, and mission in order to build organizational unity and constancy of purpose. Just as important, the leader needs to know how well the organization is meeting its purpose. Without feedback on performance, results, and success, leadership is operating in the dark when making operational and organizational decisions.

Actions taken by an organizational leader need to be informed actions. The leader needs to know specifically what the objectives are, how well the system is performing against those objectives, and what is and is not working. It is critical that shortcomings in performance be identified by the organization so the needs of the organization can be developed and determined.

Given solid evaluation data on programs, the leader is enabled to make sound, data-driven decisions. Solid evaluation data are not usually perceptual, they are objective, empirical, and replicable. The data speak for themselves. Perceptions are often skewed because of a number of factors, so clinical methods of testing assumptions about programs are necessary. Unless a program stands the test of scrutiny and evaluation of its performance, the leader is less than sure of the program's worth or value.

Strategy 21: WHY

Schools often gather data. Less often, data are scrutinized for meaning by school personnel and used in guiding action. In curriculum management audits conducted by affiliates of Curriculum Management Systems, Inc., across the United States, school systems were frequently found to have had inadequate data and information about programs and program performance. Moreover, school systems were frequently found to have misused or not used information they had in hand. Consider *Figure 16* below, which depicts evaluation data on a special reading program in an Eastern Seaboard school system.

Figure 16

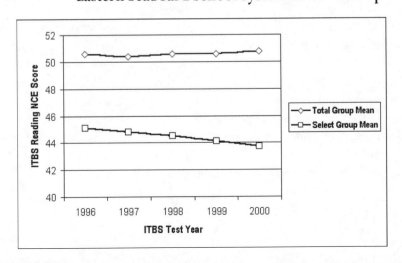

ITBS Reading Score 1996-2000
Eastern Seaboard School System Cohort Group

In *Figure 16*, data on a select group of students were gathered over a five-year period by the school system. The same students were tested annually in late spring. Over the five-year period, the select group of students produced a steady decline in performance relative to the total student group (declining norm curve equivalent position) on the reading section of the Iowa Test of Basic Skills. In the curriculum audit that revealed this information, it was noted that the school system had these data but had not disaggregated and used the data to determine whether or not their program for this select group was succeeding. It was not succeeding, but prior to the curriculum audit, the program was perceived to be successful.

The select group was comprised of approximately 530 students who were behind in reading compared to their counterparts (approximately 70,000 students were in the system) beginning in first grade. The special program placed the underperforming students in small group classes with no more than 15 or so students in the class where a regular teacher taught them. Primarily, the program was two dimensional-small classes and grouped by achievement. As seen in *Figure 16* and documented in the audit, the select group of students was not experiencing success equally with the total group of students.

Findings such as these are helpful in informing administrators of what actions to consider, what programs to keep, modify, or terminate, and what needs to address. It is easy to see the power of evaluative data–they are a very useful tool for school administrators that guide and direct decision-making, organizational improvement, and constructive action.

Strategy 21: HOW

Carrying out program evaluation to guide decisions relative to pupil achievement requires a number of specific steps and procedural activities. Specific procedural steps to follow include the following:

1. Identify and clarify what is to be measured (what significant learning objectives are being addressed in the program).
2. Develop and design evaluation strategies with a focus on feedback and improvement of student achievement against the program objectives (include all assessment items and instruments that parallel the program objectives).
3. Develop and implement a pre/post, criterion-referenced assessment procedure that documents, records, and reports student achievement against specific program objectives. Cohort groups are preferable, including use of control groups (evaluated nonparticipants in the program under study).

4. Disaggregate and analyze feedback information to evaluate differences related to gender, ethnicity, and economically disadvantaged status.
5. Note discrepancies between groups, and compare gains of all students to expectations set forth in the program objectives. Identify the scope and nature of objective achievement.
6. Communicate results to stakeholders, teachers, and others for consideration of program options, alternatives, and courses of action for improvement.
7. Use programmatic feedback data in administrative decision-making support or modify effective programs and terminate ineffective programs.

Evaluation is a simple form of accountability. If a program is purported to accomplish a specific purpose (i.e., deliver achievement of learner objectives), it is essential to determine whether or not the program is successful against its expected results. Deficiencies in accomplishing program objectives call for administrative action and curriculum leadership.

Ignorance is not bliss in underperforming schools, and neither is disregarding data about program performance and success. Competent leadership gladly welcomes the opportunity to connect measurement of results (in terms of reaching intentions) to determine how to better serve the organization's clientele and meet their learning needs.

Strategy 22

Ensure that Textbooks and Instructional Resources Are Aligned to District Curriculum Objectives and Assessments in both Content and Context Dimensions

The District has a process to ensure that textbooks and instructional resources are aligned to district objectives and assessments as well as other external assessments. Analysis includes deep alignment both at the content and context levels.

Strategy 22: WHAT

Imagine a situation where students were expected to learn certain things, but the textbook used in instruction was unrelated to the topics expected. The objective would call for one thing, but the text would deal with another. Of course that would cause considerable concern, as it should, but it is often the case in schools. Textbooks have not been shown to be well connected in content or context to standardized tests commonly used in the United States, whether they are norm- or criterion-referenced assessments. Some texts provide less than a twenty percent match with major national instruments used to test learning. Do not believe what publishers say about alignment. What they do is a very surface job of alignment. The type of alignment suggested in this book is a very substantive type of match–in both content and context.

Using a textbook as the sole mode of instructional delivery may create a situation in which the tested objectives are not taught adequately. To assure maximum alignment with the criterion of success (tested learning), it's critical that educational leaders select and selectively use textbooks and other instructional materials that parallel and match that criterion. In effect, the leader is assuring continuity between objectives (what is desired), and teaching (what and how they are taught), and what constitutes the measure of success (what is tested). Quality control demands aligning the written and tested curriculum with the taught curriculum, including textbooks and instructional resources.

Instructional resources may in and of themselves be powerful and exciting tools to use, but unless there is a connection with what is desired and what is measured, achievement will fall short of the system's intentions. It will usually take multiple resources to align with an entire course of study.

Strategy 22: WHY

High-performing schools anticipate what students are expected to know, think, do, feel, or be like, and they teach to that set of expectations. In addition, the methods and modes of measurement need to be manifested in the curriculum taught. For example, if a textbook presents a particular concept (i.e., the concept of "perimeter") in a specific manner, that manner of presentation must resemble or parallel how "perimeter" is measured in the assessment system. If there is no match or parallelism, the learners will not successfully transfer what they have encountered in the textbook to the test.

Worse yet, if the textbook leaves out the particular concept, the learners will be greatly disadvantaged when the concept is tested later. These issues would not be problematic if textbooks were better aligned, or if teachers did not depend so heavily upon textbooks for activities, content, and contexts. However, in many curriculum management audits conducted by affiliates of Curriculum Management Systems, Inc., findings indicate that teachers often do depend heavily upon textbooks for instructional use.

In some curriculum evaluations, auditors have found that tested concepts were omitted to a large extent in textbooks, some concepts were superficially treated, and some concepts were unnecessarily taught repeatedly. For example, in one curriculum management audit, the concept of "perimeter" was taught in 5th grade, 6th grade, and 7th grade, and it was tested in 8th grade. Even with such duplication, students only demonstrated 80 percent mastery at the 8th grade, largely due to a lack of match in contextual presentation (the test used hypothetical problems with complex building structures, instead of simple polygons).

Achievement is lessened when instruction includes texts and instructional resources that do not anticipate or match content, contexts, and underlying objectives measured as tested learning.

Strategy 22: HOW

The leaders of high-performing schools take steps to assure that instructional materials selected and used in their schools are adequately aligned with learner expectations, system objectives, and tested learning. To accomplish this task, the following steps are suggested:

1. Identify specifically what students are expected to learn. System objectives, measurement circumstances, structured factors, and learner expectations need to be included in the identified body of learning. This process may need to include backloading from instruments used to test learning (see Strategy 12).
2. Once the expected learning is identified, it needs to be organized by content area and grade level.
3. Selecting a content area and one grade level, the specific learner expectations are listed in table form down the first column (see *Figure 17* below) on a large chart.
4. Procure available textbooks for the selected grade level and content area (publishers are willing to provide copies for examination).
5. Create a column for each textbook (see *Figure 17* below).

Figure 17

Textbook Content/Treatment Comparisons Chart
(Use for Each Grade Level and Subject Matter Area)

Learner Concepts	Textbook A	Textbook B	Textbook C
(Example:) "Measure and accurately determine the perimeter of a multisided building."	No treatment of concept	Cut out and paste treatment of concept here	Cut out and paste treatment of concept here

Circle best treatment of concept after comparisons

6. Tear out the section of each textbook and paste its treatment of the particular expectation in its column and in the row for that expectation. Repeat until all learner concepts have corresponding textbook sections pasted in a row.

7. Compare each textbook's treatment of the learning concept. Select the textbook section that best matches the expectation for learners, and circle it in red. Repeat this step for all learner concepts and expectations.

8. Tabulate all responses, and identify the textbook that best matches the set of learner expectations for the content area and grade level selected. Also note the areas that are not addressed in the textbook. Those expectations will require other instructional materials.

9. Use the textbook that has the greatest number of matches with curriculum expectations.

(Note: It is also possible to do the textbook or instructional material matching with computer technology. Textbook sections can be scanned into a computer, catalogued, and labeled for pasting into an electronic chart. Projecting the chart on a wall screen facilitates group comparisons.)

Of course, there are several ways to compare textbook treatments of learner expectations and concepts (Muther, 1992).[4] The important thing is that the instructional leader needs to make sure that materials used in instruction are appropriate, and match and align with the specific learner concepts and expectations. Without the alignment of instructional materials, student achievement will diminish in terms of tested learning.

---

[4] See for example, Muther, C. (1990). "Selecting and Evaluating Textbooks." Chapter in Poston, W., et. al., *Making Schools Work: Practical Management of Support Services.* Newbury Park, CA: Corwin Press.

Strategy 23

Use Technology in Design or Selection Procedures to Ensure Strong Connections to System Learning Expectations and Feedback

Technology software is designed or selected based on strong alignment to the content, context, and cognitive level of the district objectives and assessments and, on its potential to enhance the quality of instruction and learning.

Strategy 23: WHAT

In the past two decades, computer-based instructional media have grown in popularity across the country, and high-end software giants have sold millions of software systems to schools for use in the classroom and in the school office. Very ambitious claims have been made on behalf of these technology programs, but little evidence has been provided to justify their use as an instructional system.

Initially, software offerings were designed to be supplementary in nature, but contemporary software packages are intended to provide a comprehensive, beginning-to-end learning scheme for students, complete with a "correlation of lesson plans" to state standards of assessment. The dilemma facing many educational leaders is that technology-based instructional programs may or may not be congruent with what students are expected to learn within a given school system. Moreover, some of the technology systems offer tempting options and alternatives for schools. Some of these newer options include the following:

- There is software that "teaches" and that requires little time of a teacher. For example, one program provides short video lessons on concepts in algebra taught by a "cybernetic teacher" via a desktop computer located in the classroom or at home. Students access their lessons individually at a computer screen and get the instruction from the computer. No teacher is required.

- Information on student performance is available for teacher diagnoses. The computer combines classroom, school, district, and state data to give teachers real-time information designed to benefit students immediately. Teachers use test scores to diagnose weaknesses or locate areas of the curriculum that have not been mastered and address them before the school year ends.

- Teachers without formal software programming can use problem-based scenarios. For example, one problem set for a science class might state that, "A dead fish washes up on shore and the students must find the source of the pollution that killed the fish, using the computer as their research tool." As students work on the problems in small groups, specially designed mapping software keeps track of the steps students take in attempting to solve each problem. The teacher can review the process students use to solve the problems, with different patterns revealing the depth of the students' grasp of the subject matter. Timely access to the mapping information lets teachers quickly adjust strategies for struggling students.

- Educators can also use computerized achievement testing to measure how students are mastering state and local curriculum standards. Combining advances in measurement theory and technology, computerized adaptive testing (CAT) provides information about the actual level of a student's achievement. CAT has the ability to customize a test to a student's achievement level. Such tests begin by asking a question at the average level. If the question is answered correctly, the computer increases the level of difficulty on the next question. When a question is answered incorrectly, the next question presented will be at or below the level of the previous question. Students at different levels of achievement in the same classroom can take different versions of the same test, versions targeted to their own achievement level.

The major issue regarding technology is not whether its spectacular claims are true-though this can be debated; the major issue is whether it is the right tool, at the right time, in the right place.

Strategy 23: WHY

There is little doubt that technology affords great and extraordinary processes and content to learners. Unfortunately, much of the time spent using technology may be on topics, content, or material that are less than optimally relevant to the learning the school system expects its students to acquire. Unless there is a strong connection between the technology and the school's needs, use of technology may undermine the aims and purposes of the system under the guise of provocative and tantalizing activities and devices.

It is a responsibility of instructional leaders to assure that technological hardware and software used in school classrooms are appropriate in both function and consequence. Much of the "Star Wars" technology observed in schools in curriculum audits has demonstrated little connection to desired learning for students. Many teachers report that students may spend hours on the computer and enjoy it to the fullest, but in the end they acquire either inadequate amounts or inappropriate types of learning.

The key question for instructional leaders in addressing software and hardware considerations is "SO WHAT?" WHAT is the result or effect or impact of using a particular type of technology? WHAT difference does it make? WHAT does it add to or how does it enhance the quality of learning measured by system assessment instruments? Unfortunately, answers to such questions are often lacking, scarce, or altogether absent.

Strategy 23: HOW

Scrutinizing technology, including devices and processes (hardware and software), requires assertive action on the part of the instructional leader. In reviewing many systems of technology in instructional media, curriculum audits have revealed that the biggest compelling factor in obtaining such systems is the availability of funds to acquire them. To avoid wasting precious resources and to assure connectivity to demonstration of learning desired by the system, the following steps are offered as suggestions on how to proceed:

1. First, determine what type of device or application is under consideration. What does it purport to offer? Unless the hardware or software manifests a strong connection between what it does and what the school system needs, it needs to be disregarded. If the proposed device or process appears to connect with documented system needs, then further consideration may be carried out.

Technology Factors to Consider:

1. *Type of device or application (Does it fit?)*
2. *Validation of results (Does it work?)*
3. *Match with expectations (Is it congruent?)*
4. *Documentation within system (Pilot test?)*
5. *Content, context, cognitive level (What's the nature?)*
6. *Cost-benefit (What worth or value?)*

2. Next, clearly identify validation that confirms that the technology in fact delivers what it promises. What studies are provided that confirm the technology's capabilities and results (and how good were they)? Without validation information, technology may be promising something it cannot and will not deliver. Of course, the school leader needs to discern validity and reliability of research. For example, if the manufacturer is using its own research to demonstrate the value of the technology, such information is less valuable than external, third party, independent research.

3. Then, proceed to determine the match between the technology and the school system's desired learning expectations for students. Is the technology a process or does it deliver a product? The leader must determine if the process is congruent with system procedures and policies. The leader must confirm that the product delivered is congruent with what the school system expects its clientele to acquire. Without such congruence or confirmation, the technology may disjoin the instructional integrity of the system.

4. Further, document the content and context of the technology as to how and where it fits within the system's curriculum. What tested learning does it purport to deliver? Review processes such as pilot-studies, etc must experimentally validate such expectations. The educational leader must provide assurance that the technology does in fact deliver curriculum content or context consistent with system expectations.

5. Another key step is to determine the cognitive level of the content and context of the technology applications or apparatus. Given use of the technology, what level of thinking is addressed when students use it? Some technology software has been found to be very simplistic and fundamental in its cognitive level. The instructional leader must prevent adverse consequences resulting from the use of

low-level activities or devices and ensure that the technology promulgates complex, high-order thinking and problem-solving levels congruent with system requirements.

6. Finally, the instructional leader must determine if the technology is worth its cost. How much does it cost, and is it a good use of system funds? Much technology is very expensive, and the benefits are often less than clear. It is critical for the costs to be tabulated and then evaluated against system priorities and needs to see if the expenditure is appropriate or justified. In most cases, school systems may find that the consumption of scarce system financial resources in acquiring and maintaining technology is not worth it. Determining ahead of time what benefits accrue to the system, and how those benefits meet the needs of the system, will help in deciding whether to support and expend the cost amount.

Technology offers much for schools; however, it does not guarantee learning. What the system needs, requires, desires, and seeks should drive all decisions for acquisition of materiel of all types. Otherwise scarce resources may not be used to best advantage in fostering achievement for students in the system.

Strategy 24

Provide Training in the Use of Instructional Resources and Their Alignment with System Curriculum Objectives-Content, Context, and Cognitive Level

Staff members have been provided quality training on the use of instructional resources in alignment with district objectives–focusing on the content, context, and cognitive level of the objectives (or external assessments).

Strategy 24: WHAT

It is one thing to have organizational purposes; it is quite another to carry out those purposes. Often faculty and staff need training on the nature and purpose of organizational goals as well as training on how to accomplish these goals. Without strategies, methods, or approaches-without training-personnel will flounder in their efforts to initiate improvement. They may even cease to progress at all.

Assumptions about the readiness of personnel to undertake any change or process in order to reach an organization's goals are often mistaken. Change requires considerable time, planning, and training for its initiation, and the educational leader is responsible for meeting the needs of personnel during this process.

In overcoming factors that contribute to underperforming schools, training in the area of alignment is essential. Instructional resources used by teachers in the classroom must be congruent with the goals and objectives addressed, and all resources must be equivalent in content, context, and cognitive level in order to be used effectively. For example, learning how to read and use a map to find your way to a previously unknown destination is a high-level cognitive objective. Memorizing the capitals of the states shown on the maps (a low-level cognitive skill) would be incongruent with the former objective and not germane to the learning.

Teachers need to be able to discern the specific skills dealt with in instructional materials and determine if the skills are equivalent in content, context, and cognitive level to the system's learner expectations. Such discernment and determinations require training and development.

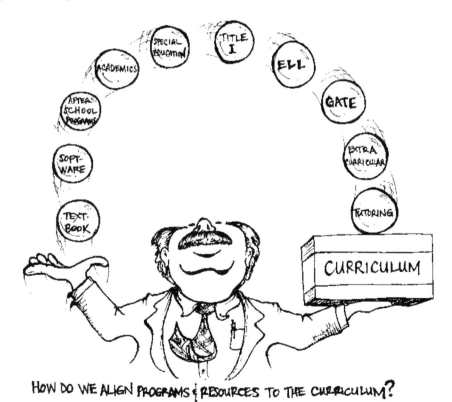

HOW DO WE ALIGN PROGRAMS & RESOURCES TO THE CURRICULUM?

Strategy 24: WHY

High-performing schools should focus on all dimensions of their operations–time, materials, activities, sequence, etc.-while always keeping the mission and expected results of the system's curriculum in mind. Focusing on all dimensions creates greater harmony in the organizational effort and ensures a greater degree of success. This "harmonizing" process is referred to as "optimization in organizational quality improvement." With all forces and actions headed in the same direction, the organization has an opportunity to gain momentum and accomplishment from its efforts.

In teaching, many factors collide with learning. Use of time can affect the level of learning, specificity of content presented can impact the quality of learning, and parallel contextual frames can improve the nature of learning. However, curriculum audits have found that much of the classroom activity observed is largely undirected, unfocused, and haphazard in implementation. To overcome such ineffectiveness and to obtain greater organizational focus, training of personnel is required.

Strategy 24: HOW

Instructional leaders create the conditions for effective staff development and training. Several suggestions follow for consideration:

1. The school leader needs to foster an expectation of professional growth. Much of this is accomplished through his or her own self-directed professional growth and development. In effect, the leader models good professional growth.

2. All training for personnel needs to be based on a careful analysis of data and must be data-driven. Training for individual teachers needs to be different and in accordance with individual needs. No "shotgun" or one-size-fits-all approach should be used. Careful diagnosis of needs and provision of matching training should be commonplace.

3. Training efforts must be extrapolated from district goals and instructional priorities (policy, plans, etc.), and focus on proven research-based approaches that have shown to increase productivity.

4. To be successful, training must be based on valid theories of human learning and development and adult learning, use a variety of staff development approaches, and be matched with the individual diagnosed needs.

5. Next, the system's curriculum expectations need to be organized by grade level and content area to inform teachers what is to be taught at each juncture. Content, context, and cognitive level are to be included. A large chart is often helpful in this task (see *Figure 18* below).

Figure 18

Matrix of Learner Objectives and Grade Levels
Sample Reading and Language Arts Objectives

Grade Level	Content	Context	Level of Cognition
K	(Sample) Recognize letters of the alphabet and demonstrate the correct sound for each letter	Nomenclature of alphabet letters	Comprehension
1	(Sample) Decode and explain the meaning of short passages with simple words.	Interpretation of meaning (sequenced with individual reading)	Application
2	(Sample) Read and identify the main characters of a short youth adventure book.	Character interpretation	Analysis and application
Etc. ⇩	Etc. ⇩	Etc. ⇩	Etc. ⇩

6. Finally, training needs to include feedback from assessment to identify how well the specific learning expectations are being met by the system.

Appropriate training in alignment frees up the educational leader's time by giving each member of the instructional team the skills to implement alignment of the curriculum expectations and content, context, and cognitive levels accordingly. Delegation of the skill to the classroom level produces great dividends in assuring better adherence to what the system requires in terms of learning.

Strategy 25

Select or Modify Instructional Resources for Lessons to Ensure Full Alignment with System Objectives and Tested Learning

Teachers select or modify instructional resources for lessons to ensure 100% alignment with the content and context of the district objectives and assessments, including external assessments.

Strategy 25: WHAT

Many instructional materials are commercially produced, but most of the commercially products do not fit easily into local educational environments or suit the learner expectations of a given system. Resources used in the classroom are often locally developed or modified in order to fit the needs of a local community's clientele and curriculum.

Teachers must teach what is assessed, and, they must teach according to the established objectives. In order to do this, materials and instructional resources may have to be modified or created to provide suitable instructional support for the unique curriculum.

Strategy 25: WHY

If instructional resources are not germane to the system's curriculum expectations and do not match content, context, and cognitive levels, then students will not perform well on the assessment. Commercial materials are designed to address a very wide audience and often claim to meet the needs of all school systems.

School systems are unique and distinctive, particularly in terms of the varying needs of each system's clientele. Instructional resources and materials need to be modified to match the nature of the system's clientele, to support instruction related to student performance on assessments, and to give teachers appropriate tools for use in the classroom.

Strategy 25: HOW

The following steps are recommended to achieve this strategy:

1. First, identify the nature of individual learner expectations in all grade levels and in all content areas. This might be accomplished by backloading from the assessment process used by the system.

2. Next, review student results against those expectations, and ask teachers to review those areas that demonstrate inadequate achievement or student success.

3. Recommend that teachers problem-solve possible reasons for inadequate performance, and identify likely options and alternatives for improvement. Separate out all those areas that are due to improper or impotent instructional resources.

4. With the list generated from step number three above, recommend that teachers be provided with time and materials to develop instructional resources to close the gaps, and that they be requested to develop appropriate materials or modify existing resources. Teachers may need support to get this task completed and at some time other than during the school year.

5. Resources developed or modified by teachers must be inventoried, reproduced, and maintained by the system. Modified or developed resources need to be shared with all teachers in comparable content areas and grade levels.

Opportunities to adapt instructional resources to local system needs and curriculum expectations will enhance alignment of resources with the tested curriculum and contribute dramatically to student achievement improvement.

Strategy 26

Place Students in Programs and Activit.
in an Equitable Manner and with
Equal Access to the Curriculum

Students are placed in programs/activities in an equitable
matter with equal access to the curriculum.

Strategy 26: WHAT

A well-managed school system reflects a strong commitment to both consistency and equity. *Equity* is defined as the state, action, or principle of treating people in accordance with differentiated needs. This contrasts to the notion of *equality*, which is the quality, or condition of being the same as something else. Equity and fairness to all students is expected in all areas including student placement, course access, program opportunities, etc.

Equity is an elusive concept and difficult to achieve. However, a high-performing school system makes sure to adjust its instructional responses to the different students and provides different educational treatments to meet those individual needs. Research shows that low-performing school systems allocating resources and assigning educational responses generally on the basis of student enrollment counts rather than on measured needs.

Strategy 26: WHY

Different needs require different treatments. Treating students the same when their characteristics and needs are different is often unfair and inappropriate. If one child has not learned to read adequately by the 3rd grade, that child needs different instruction than the other students. Greater intensification, extension, or specialized instructional support or settings may be called for in such a case. Failing to acknowledge and differentiate instruction according to needs will prevent opportunities for students to overcome their circumstances.

Figure 19 below was extrapolated from a midwestern school system's curriculum audit report and serves as an example of how equity applies to schools. Achievement across schools was obviously different. That would be no surprise, as some variation is normal. However, students were achieving success in uneven ways, and that would not be normal.

Figure 19

3rd Grade Reading Achievement Differences by School
Midwestern School District Elementary Schools

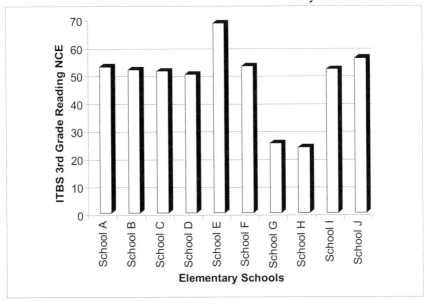

In *Figure 19* above, it is evident that School G and School H are underperforming schools. That was no surprise–nearly every school system of any size has a few schools that do not perform up to the levels of other schools. The surprise was that the two schools were treated identically to the other schools. They received the same per-pupil allocation of funding, the same number of students per teacher, the same materials and textbooks, and the same instructional support as other schools on a per-pupil basis. Such a condition is inequitable, since no differentiation is made in terms of different student needs.

Without accommodation of different needs, underperforming schools would have little likelihood of closing the gap with other schools. In the case above, the school system took measures to overcome the gaps and the discrepancies in achievement between the schools. The two underperforming schools received an additional $100,000 each (all schools were about the same size) for reading program augmentation.

Special teachers were obtained to deal with the reading deficits, and their duties included the following:

- Diagnosing individual student reading achievement against system learner objectives. Provide specific information on individual students on a daily basis to teachers for use in prescribing different reading activities for students with low achievement.

- Preparing and maintaining an extensive collection of special instructional resources for use in classrooms with underperforming students that were designed to enhance reading achievement.
- Disaggregate assessment information about achievement against system reading objectives for use in identifying curriculum areas not being adequately taught.
- Provide staff development to teachers on how to better address the critical needs in reading of underperforming students.
- Individually tutor chronically underperforming students in reading by use of a program utilizing external volunteers to assist classroom teachers.

Given this differential treatment of students with different needs, there was good news-the two underperforming schools began to show achievement gains immediately, and after three years, the achievement gap between schools had been diminished substantially.

The point is a simple one—different needs require different responses and treatments in instruction. Treating all students with equal resources and equal treatments when the students are unequal in terms of learning is inequitable and unjust. No society can afford to resign itself to such a large incidence of failure among its school clientele.

Strategy 26: HOW

School organizations tend to be very conscious of promoting equality and of being seen as agents of equality, particularly in the area of resource allocation. Equal allocations in organizations responding to diverse needs, however, do not promote equity. School districts committed to overcoming the ill effects of inequity devise and implement strategies that create a climate of high expectations for all students regardless of race, gender, or home background. Instructional leaders monitor instruction to ensure that the delivery of instruction reflects a clear understanding of how different children learn.

Try these suggestions to overcome learning deficits for students with diverse needs in underperforming schools:

1. The governing body needs to support the school sites in their efforts to meet the needs of different students. Allocation of resources needs to follow the needs of individual schools, and within a school in accordance with different needs of pupils. The governing body needs to select, adopt, and allocate instructional and human resources across schools to provide impact on schools in a consistent and equitable manner *based on need*.

2. Staff development and parental education needs to be geared toward enhancing the community's beliefs in the difference of needs and skills, and toward a commitment to reach and achieve success with all students.

3. After diagnosing the needs of different student groups, undertake a comprehensive effort to modify or terminate programs that are creating major issues impacting ethnicity and gender.

4. Modify course offerings and improve access to courses to enhance consistency and equity.

5. Develop procedures and monitor the implementation of processes that foster comparability across school sites and grade levels.

6. Develop and implement a research-based program of instruction supported by staff development that capitalizes on the strengths of all students.

7. Develop a five-year comprehensive staff development plan that focuses on the delivery of the curriculum to all students. Monitor the use of strategies with periodic assessment of the effectiveness of the staff development in increasing student learning.

8. Devise assessment strategies that consider not only the analytical skills of student but that also support and encourage the creative, practical, and social skills of all students.

9. Take assertive action to disaggregate assessment data to pinpoint specific learning skill deficits, and realign instruction to better address those differential needs in the classroom. Monitor results on a weekly basis against the system's learning objectives.

Doing the same things for all students and expecting different results is impractical and futile. To overcome differences among learners, different approaches, strategies, and efforts are called for, particularly in assuring alignment of instruction with feedback from assessment instruments. Gaps among learners are simply the result of individual differences, and gaps can be overcome given appropriate action and confidence in differentiated educational remedies.

Strategy 27

Implement Effective Programs and Strategies with English Language Learners

Effective programs and strategies for working with students whose primary language is not English are in place to focus on vocabulary development and reading comprehension approaches.

Strategy 27: WHAT

Many schools have students whose first language is not English. It is critical that these schools use effective programs and strategies for working with students whose primary language is not English and that they focus on vocabulary development and reading comprehension approaches. Language diversity in many schools has reached substantive levels unprecedented in U.S. schools in recent years. To meet the needs of these students, a systematic, comprehensive approach is advised. It can be a part of a bilingual program (using two languages of instruction in the student's schooling) but it this not the only possibility. School systems offer a variety of programs to students including ESL (English as a Second Language), "sheltered" English, "immersion," all or part day, pullout programs, summer extension, extended day, etc.

English Language Learners may be offered any or all of the program options available. In English as a Second Language, a systematic approach following specific methodologies for learning English is used. Sheltered English programs provide instruction for nonnative speakers in a way adapted to the students' English proficiency levels. Immersion programs place students in a totally English-speaking environment, without any use of their native language. Students learn from constant and perpetual exposure to the English language via visual, aural, oral, and tactile means. Many programs are time-extending programs that give students additional time to acquire the English language.

There are many things teachers and principals can do to help non-English speaking children in school. First, it is important to recognize and accept that placement with peers is desirable for many reasons, but it is unrealistic to assume that students new to English can learn it fast enough to keep up with their peers for the first year or two. Prior learning in the student's native language is a major factor. If their proficiency includes facility with an alphabet and Latin/European characters, it will be easier for them to learn English. Other demographic factors play a part as well, just as they do with English-speaking children, including parental educational level, living conditions, parental relationships, etc. A critical factor is the attitude and response of the host society (the child's home school) in regard to the student's language and needs.

Strategy 27: WHY

It goes without saying that children of all cultures have differential social, cognitive, physical, emotional, and language needs. The complex assortment of issues related to placing English Language Learners (ELL) must not be overlooked in placement decisions. Integration and/or immersion may force students to compromise their total education just to acquire minimal skills. Once intermediate skills are acquired, students may more fully participate in classroom activities in English.

Teachers and classroom situations must be fully ready for the cultural diversity and learning challenge that non-English-speaking students present. The more the teachers are trained, the better. The more other students readily accept and help ELL students, the better. The more the school reaches out to parents and the child's home, the better. Teachers need to understand that a child's diminished ability to work in English may not reflect the child's intellectual capacities. Teachers who have high expectations, competence in classroom instruction for ELL students, and sensitivity to children's needs make a big difference in the success of ELL students.

Bilingual education avoids the "sink or swim" approach which can be very successful, but only if students are being instructed increasingly in English, and only if adequate attention is given to their native language to maintain proficiency. The goal is proficiency in both languages and for skills to transfer from one language to the next. However, when bilingual programs are not viable, the best alternative is to provide students with comprehensive, specially designed instruction in English *(Alexandrowicz, 2000).*[5]

Strategy 27: HOW

Ideally, students are permitted to add a second language to their native language in speaking, reading, and writing *(Alexandrowicz, 2000).*[6] The aim is for students to become literate in two languages and to move from instruction in their own tongue until they are proficient enough to transfer to regular classrooms. By the time students reach middle school age, they are proficient enough to be taught exclusively in English, except, of course, for a language arts component used to strengthen their own language. What administrators need to know is that acquisition of skills and knowledge in one language obviates the necessity for learning those things again in another language.

In "English Only" situations (where bilingual education is not allowed), the educational community needs to continue to identify individual student needs as well as the available alternatives and courses of action and how to best meet those need. Collaborative involvement of the home and community in such decision-making is helpful

Instruction for ELL students calls for special staff development for faculty and staff. Faculty need to have training in the area of second language acquisition, cultural diversity engagement and interactions, and classroom management in classrooms with a wide spectrum of intellectual, academic, and language backgrounds. Well trained teachers exemplify the highest levels of competency in lesson delivery. Directions and explanations need to be carefully delivered so as to meet the needs of second language learners. Using graphics, pictures, and other nonverbal clues are helpful. In addition, careful planning in the use of vocabulary and instructions must include repetition and paraphrasing to help the student gain understanding of what is expected. Teachers need to focus on critical thinking and hold realistic expectations for academic interactions with ELL students. Lowering expectations is detrimental to ELL students just as it is for any student.

The principal must model the highest commitment to building a community in which ELL learners, teachers, parents, students, and others work together harmoniously and where respect permeates through all activity. Given effective approaches and commitment, any child–ELL or otherwise–can succeed in school.

---

[5] Alexandrowicz, V. (2000). In Cunningham, W. and Cordeiro, P. *Educational Administration: A Problem-Based Approach* (Boston: Allyn and Bacon), 110-112.
[6] *Ibid.*

ꝏ Analysis of Standard Three ꝏ

Now it is time for you to evaluate the status of your school or school district on *Standard Three: Align Program and Instructional Resources to the Curriculum and Provide Student Equality and Equity*. What is the status of your situation regarding these strategies and what changes are needed? Write your responses in the spaces provided.

STRATEGY	CURRENT STATUS	CHANGES NEEDED
19. Align Programs to the Curriculum to Ensure Congruity	❏Adequate ❏Not adequate	
20. Use Research and Data that Document Results to Drive Program Selection, and Validate the Implementation of Programs with Action Research	❏Adequate ❏Not adequate	
21. Evaluate Programs to Determine Effectiveness to Strengthen Student Achievement of Curriculum Objectives	❏Adequate ❏Not adequate	
22. Ensure Textbooks and Instructional Resources Are Aligned to the District Curriculum Objectives and Assessments in both Content and Context Dimensions	❏Adequate ❏Not adequate	
23. Use Technology in Design or Selection Procedures to Ensure Strong Connections to System Learning Expectations and Feedback	❏Adequate ❏Not adequate	
24. Provide Training in the Use of Instructional Resources and Their Alignment with System Curriculum Objectives (Content, Context, Cognitive Level)	❏Adequate ❏Not adequate	

❧ Analysis of Standard Three, Continued

STRATEGY	CURRENT STATUS	CHANGES NEEDED
25. Select or Modify Instructional Resources for Lessons to Ensure Full Alignment with System Objectives and Tested Learning	❏ Adequate ❏ Not adequate	
26. Place Students in Programs and Activities in an Equitable Manner and with Equal Access to the Curriculum	❏ Adequate ❏ Not adequate	
27. Implement Effective Programs and Strategies with English Language Learners	❏ Adequate ❏ Not adequate	

4

STANDARD FOUR

Use a Mastery Learning Approach
and Effective Teaching Strategies

The following presents seven highly powerful strategies regarding the teaching process:

28. *Implement a Mastery Learning Model*

29. *Align Teaching to the Curriculum*

30. *Provide Differentiated Instruction*

31. *Provide Practice to Master the Curriculum*

32. *Use Effective Teaching Practices*

33. *Provide Students with Differentiated Time to Learn*

34. *Establish Individual Learning Plans for Low-Achieving Students*

Strategy 28

Implement a Master-Learning Model

*School-based administrators and all instructional staff have
been trained in the mastery teaching model and use it.*

Strategy 28: WHAT

Raising student achievement scores can be accomplished using a conceptually simple formula. Teach what you test, teach it the way you test it, and vary teaching methodology accordingly so that mastery is assured. Putting this formula on paper is easy, but we all know how difficult it can be to implement this type of process in both a consistent and persistent manner. The "teach what you test" and "teach it the way you test it" sections have been covered in other portions of this book. This segment focuses on the last part of the formula–"vary teaching methodologies accordingly so that mastery is assured."

While Strategy 28 calls for administrators and teachers to be trained in the mastery-learning model, the more important task is the full implementation of mastery-learning in the classroom. Training alone will only produce administrators and teachers who "talk the talk" but produce few results. The installation and institutionalization of a mastery-learning model is crucial to creating a learning environment where students experience classroom parallelism.

The learning of students and their continuous progress toward district standards and objectives is the central focus of an instructional model. This does not mean dictating the exact strategies a teacher is to use to teach a specific objective. Rather, it means to direct the structure for the overall delivery of instruction.

The best research model has been around for over thirty years, yet its use is sporadic in most schools across the nation. Fisher and others designed a data-driven mastery-learning model in the early seventies. It is designed to differentiate instruction. As we begin the twenty-first century, it is still the best-researched model around. *Figure 20* illustrates the basic components of the mastery-learning model as originally developed by Fisher, Bloom, Carroll, et. al.

Figure 20

Mastery Learning Model

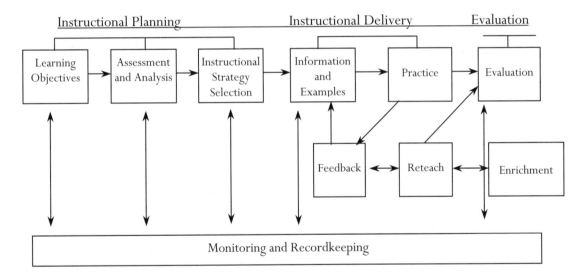

The following is a brief explanation of each component *(Downey, 2001)*[7]:

Instructional Planning
1. **Specify and order the learner objectives.** The first function in instructional planning is to identify the learner objectives in terms of what a student will know and be able to do. This is really a product of curriculum design, so it is an expectation that teachers will select and order the lesson

---

[7] Excerpt from Downey, Carolyn, "Are Your Expectations Clear Regarding an Instructional Model," Thrust, Association of California School Administrators, Burlingame, California Fall 2001.

objectives from the expected district standards and objectives to ensure alignment of the written and taught curriculum.

2. **Assess and analyze student learning on the proposed objectives.** Here diagnostic assessments are used to determine each student's status in relationship to the identified objectives selected in Step 1.

3. **Design and/or select instructional strategies.** Next, the teacher plans according to the interaction of the specified curricular objectives, the teacher assessed each student's needs, and the instructional strategies that are likely to lead to durable learning in the most effective manner. This is often called lesson design.

Instructional Delivery

4. **Provide or generate information and examples that directly correspond to the specified learning objective.** The information and examples may be conveyed in numerous ways. The key is whether the students have that which they need to master the specific objective.

5. **Provide practice for acquisition and mastery of the learning objective.** How a student responds to initial instruction influences our selection of practice opportunities. Practice opportunities vary by amount, duration, distribution, and meaningfulness.

6. **Monitor student learning on the objectives.** This component occurs throughout teaching events. Monitoring strategies include examining student participation and products. Effective monitoring is continuous, guiding future teacher planning and also shaping immediate teacher responses for each student.

7. **Furnish feedback to students on their status on each objective.** The purpose of feedback is to alert the student to both the accuracy and completeness of his/her response. Feedback should be timely and limited to student's learning needs.

8. **Reteach or provide enrichment activities as needed.** Guided by the information obtained during continuous monitoring and the analysis of this information, the teacher determines whether to begin teaching a new learning, reteach the current learning objective, or provide an enrichment opportunity for each student.

Evaluation

9. **Assess student learning throughout the instructional process.** Evaluation involves comparison of the student's status to the desired objective. The day-to-day assessments of students' responses to the delivery of instruction

provide the data to determine whether a student has acquired the learning as well as mastered the learning.

Strategy 28: WHY

Many studies have pointed out the power of the mastery-learning model *(Bloom, 1999)*[8] and the benefits accrued for student learning when teachers consistently use a mastery-learning model. The mastery-learning model provides benefits for teachers too; increased confidence and satisfaction with their teaching, more equal and equitable treatment of students, use of feedback from student learning to assess the effectiveness of their teaching are just a few.

Mastery learning assures teachers and administrators that students have been taught *and have learned* the essential skills, knowledge, and processes that are required to do well on the assessment in use in a district. High-performing schools want their students to experience "no surprises" when confronted with problems and items on any given test. No surprises means that students are well prepared to make maximum transfer from what they have learned in the classroom to a situation or problem on a test. Maximum transfer means that students have experienced similar types of problems and situations while engaged in learning activities in the classroom. Teachers must structure teaching episodes to parallel the types of learnings students will encounter on a test.

Mastery learning connects the written curriculum to the tested curriculum. It focuses the emphasis of teaching and learning on those learnings that the student and the school system will be held accountable to in a testing program.

When mastery-learning is not employed by the teaching staff, the element of surprise is much more prevalent. Surprise means that students are encountering problems or concepts of an unfamiliar nature on tests. Unfamiliarity hinders speed and accuracy–both of which are critical elements to student performance on most state tests or norm-referenced tests. Surprise and unfamiliarity hinder students from low socioeconomic backgrounds in particular. These students are most impacted by a lack of parallelism in classroom teaching.

Strategy Twenty-eight: HOW:

Traditional staff development in implementing the mastery-learning model will not suffice. Traditional staff development does not contain the intensity, duration, or follow-

---

[8] Bloom, Benjamin S. (1999). *"The Search for Methods of Instruction."* Chapter in Ornstein, Allan C. and Behar-Horenstein, Linda S., et.al., *Contemporary Issues in Curriculum.* Needham Heights, MA: Allyn and Bacon.

up components necessary to change participant behavior. If teacher behaviors aren't adequately addressed, then it is likely that the participants will do what they have always done once back in the classroom. Staff development in the mastery-learning model must include a component requiring follow-up and on-the-job application of the skills and processes of the model. Specifically, training administrators and teachers in the use of the mastery-learning model must include:

1. A well-designed plan for the development of teachers and administrators on the mastery-learning model. The plan should include a needs assessment of the existing skills, knowledge, and experiences of the staff in using the mastery-learning model.

2. A sequencing of staff development sessions that provides for input, practice, and reflection on the stages and techniques of a mastery-learning model. Sequencing should include multiple sessions for staff development, each followed by practice time back in the classroom. If possible, each participant would have the instructor of the staff development program (or someone trained in the model) come to the classroom to provide constructive feedback on one or more practice sessions.

3. A clearly delineated expectation from the board and the administration that mastery-learning is the norm of the district and that all teachers and administrators are expected to employ this methodology in day-to-day classroom instruction.

4. Incorporation of mastery-learning into the standards of performance for staff appraisal.

5. Data collected from assessments of student achievement, which are used to determine the effectiveness of the instructional program in general, and implementation of a mastery-learning model specifically.

6. An ongoing training component as part of the staff development program. Teachers or administrators who need additional assistance and training are provided ample opportunity to receive the assistance they need. The success of the mastery-learning staff development effort will be measured in part by the degree of mastery attained by the participants in implementing the model.

To increase student achievement, school districts and individual schools must do something different from what they have done in the past. The mastery-learning model is one tool that can be used to ensure that teachers are well prepared to teach the aligned district curriculum. If teachers teach what is tested, teach it the way it is tested, and employ the mastery-learning model so that student mastery is attained, higher test scores will result.

Strategy 29

Align Teaching to the Curriculum

Teachers and other instructional staff align their teaching to the content, cognitive level, and context specified by the district objectives and/or other external assessments, especially if the district objectives do not have this type of precision.

Strategy 29: WHAT

An important consideration in raising student achievement is the extent to which the district has an aligned written, taught, and tested curriculum. Each component is an essential part of designing an instructional program to match the extant accountability system in place (i.e., state test, district designed/adopted tests, etc.). A first step in this process is the design of a curriculum that is aligned to the tests in use (see Strategy 1). This assures that the written curriculum is congruent with what is being assessed on external tests while internal tests are aligned to the district's written curriculum.

Measured learning is greatly enhanced by teacher adherence to a written, aligned, and articulated curriculum that promotes continuity and cumulative acquisition of skills and knowledge from grade to grade and school to school. This strategy is about curriculum delivery—teachers ensuring that the learnings they are teaching to are the designed and written curriculum student learnings. Taught curriculum is the learnings taught when the teacher teaches. This strategy is about the nonnegotiable curriculum teachers are to teach. They still have the flexibility to determine the means toward students' achievement of the learnings.

The written curriculum in a school district is the statement of priorities and shows the emphasis the district has placed on various parts of the curriculum. Adopted by the Board of Education, the written curriculum becomes the officially sanctioned content for curriculum delivery. Implementation of the official curriculum is the responsibility of each teacher in the system.

The school district has the right and responsibility to clearly state the expectation that teachers use the approved curriculum. Teachers have a right to know what those expectations are and how they will affect their teaching. Learning expectations should be clear and explicit regarding the content, context, and cognitive levels teachers are to employ in the classroom. The district is responsible for assuring continuity and equality of access across the system in the delivery of the curriculum and for equitable delivery for each student (see Strategy 26). It does this through the consistent delivery of the curriculum by each teacher across grades and schools.

The Board of Education, through its policy-making authority, establishes the expectation for teaching the prescribed curriculum. Policy should be clear and direct regarding the actions of teachers in the system. Policy should be directive rather than descriptive. Board policy becomes the framework to guide and direct the professional staff in the delivery of the curriculum.

Strategy 29: WHY

Teaching not aligned to the written curriculum may fragment the learnings of students so that their educational experience does not match the types of skills, knowledge, and processes they will encounter on external and internal assessments. Not teaching the aligned curriculum may skew teaching so that students are spending excessive amounts of time learning skills, knowledge, or processes deemphasized on the test and the district curriculum, while not receiving the appropriate instruction on items emphasized on assessments and in district curriculum expectations.

High-performing schools and school districts direct teaching to the expected set of performance standards that enable students to succeed on tests. Aligning teaching to the curriculum just makes sense. It makes sense from the point of view of the student and from the point of view of the teacher and administrator. It is totally consistent with the notion of "teach what you test, teach it the way you test it, and vary teaching methodology accordingly so that mastery is assured"—elements leading to "no surprises" for students.

One other note on Why to use Strategy 29: if the Board of Education has officially adopted the curriculum of the district, as is called for in this book, then teaching the prescribed district curriculum is congruent with board policy. Not teaching the board-adopted curriculum constitutes insubordination. Board adoption of the curriculum establishes the equivalent of "law" for the district. It states clearly what is expected of the teaching staff relative to the delivery of curriculum. There is good reason why the authors emphasize the board adopting the curriculum. It ensures that the adopted curriculum will be the delivered curriculum and that the written, taught, and tested curriculum is congruent.

Strategy 29: HOW

High-performing school systems have clearly communicated expectations for the delivery of the curriculum. Teachers and administrators are well aware of what those expectations are and their roles in implementing the curriculum. High-performing systems take the necessary steps to ensure that what is taught in the classroom is consistent with the written and tested curriculum.

Curriculum leaders in school districts take actions to establish procedures to monitor the delivery of curriculum at the school site level. The following steps are suggested:

District Level
1. Design and implement administrative regulations or procedures to fully implement board policy relating to the delivery of curriculum.
2. Communicate clearly expectations to administrators and teachers about the delivery of curriculum.
3. Develop and implement administrator staff development on monitoring the curriculum. Principals in particular must be skilled in monitoring the curriculum and teaching methodology. "Walk-through" training for principals is strongly recommended. Make monitoring part of the job performance for all administrators. Central office administrators should focus on working with principals to increase their capacity to monitor curriculum and work with teachers. Those persons who evaluate principals should have as part of their job description and duties the responsibility for "monitoring the monitors."
4. Report periodically the status of teaching in the district—both from the point of view of pedagogy and delivery of the adopted curriculum.

School Level

5. Communicate clearly to teachers the expectation that the aligned curriculum is to be delivered in the classroom. Work with teachers who may have concerns about abandoning past practices and "pet projects." Help them understand the benefits for students and the school when the aligned written curriculum is taught in the classroom.

6. Inform teachers that an administrator will be in their room on a frequent basis to monitor the delivery of the curriculum and to observe teaching. The practice of "managing by wandering around" will provide a solid base for principals to use in working with teachers to increase their capacity to deliver the curriculum.

7. Establish the expectation with office personnel and others that the principal will be out in classrooms on a frequent basis and that only "true" emergencies should supersede that activity.

8. Manage time wisely. Administrators should use time spent in moving from one part of the building to another as an opportunity to drop in on classrooms. It only takes minutes to monitor curriculum and teaching in a classroom, and the benefits far outweigh any inconvenience. Skills in conducting classroom walk-throughs are crucial for any building administrator.

9. Develop a working rapport with teachers that enables them to reflect on their own teaching practices. Encourage teachers to critically analyze their own teaching behaviors to see if there are areas for growth in pedagogy or delivery of the aligned curriculum.

10. Align site-based staff development efforts to focus on areas identified by building administrators and elicit teacher self-reflection as needed for curriculum delivery or teaching methodology.

Teaching the aligned curriculum is an essential element in improving student achievement. High-performing schools and school districts have clear policy, clear expectations for the delivery of curriculum, and systems in place to monitor curriculum delivery and to make appropriate adjustments in curriculum or teaching.

Strategy 30

Provide Differentiated Instruction

Teachers and other instructional staff modify their instruction based on ongoing diagnostic assessments, provide differentiated instruction based on student learning needs, and teach prerequisite knowledge as needed.

Strategy 30: WHAT

Effective teachers are constantly aware of the instructional needs of their students, and they make appropriate modifications in their teaching to maximize the learning for each student. These teachers have devised many ways of assessing what students learn encouraging individual students to strive for mastery. Effective teachers have become experts at diagnosing the needs of students by using a variety of assessments and by bringing to bear all of the resources, experience, and methods they can in the delivery of the aligned curriculum.

Effective teachers are aware of the expectations and requirements for students as they encounter the curriculum. They use the district-adopted curriculum as a tool to focus their teaching efforts in order to get the maximum benefit from the teaching/learning time. Effective teachers have developed and honed their teaching skills to the point that they have many alternative approaches to choose from for any given teaching episode. They are continually seeking improved methods to approach teaching in the classroom and base their effectiveness on the learning accrued by their students.

Less effective teachers have few options when putting together lessons for the classroom. Their array of methods does not permit differentiated instructional approaches based on the individual needs of students, so they teach to the middle and hope that as many as possible will "get it". Less effective teachers do not employ a variety of assessment methods to ascertain the learning levels of student, and they tend not to make modifications in what they do even though feedback from student assessments is available.

High-performing schools and school districts foster a norm of teaching that includes the ability to provide differentiated instruction for students based on individual needs. These schools and districts develop these skills through staff development and actively seek out teacher candidates to fill positions who have demonstrated differentiated teaching skills.

Strategy 30: WHY

Differentiating instruction based on the needs of students increases the likelihood that students will master the essential learnings of the curriculum and perform well on district designed or adopted tests and external assessments. Differentiated instruction makes maximum use of time, instructional resources, and teaching methodologies to strive for mastery-learning on the part of all students. The intent of teaching should be student learning rather than content coverage. The role of the teacher is master technician and manager of the curriculum to direct student learning.

High-performing schools and school districts have adopted specific strategies to develop and nurture teachers who have the abilities to differentiate their teaching to the needs of students. Staff development programs, formal and informal reward systems, teacher appraisal criteria, and school and district effectiveness are in place to foster the abilities of teachers to differentiate their teaching to the individual needs of students.

Strategy 30: HOW

Instituting and institutionalizing differentiated instruction requires a number of steps. These include the following:

1. Establish a school board policy that requires differentiated instruction of all teachers in the district.
2. Clearly communicate definitions and expectations to all members of the instructional staff.
3. Provide comprehensive staff development for teachers and administrators on differentiated instruction. Provide on-the-job application and follow-up

components to ensure full implementation. Provide frequent refreshers that allow teachers to hone existing skills and learn new ones.

4. Monitor teaching methods on a frequent basis. Regular and frequent classroom walk-throughs by administrators will provide a basis for working with teachers on their skills, knowledge, and techniques of differentiated instruction. Teacher reflection on their own teaching techniques is a highly effective way for teachers to be self-motivated in modifying what they do in the classroom.

5. Use data for feedback to inform teachers, schools, and the district on the effectiveness of the instructional program. Use of data for decision-making should become the standard of performance for all levels (teachers, schools, district) of the instructional program.

Differentiating instruction to the needs of students creates the norm that the individual teacher, school, and school district expect high levels of learning from all students. It makes a definitive statement about the values of the system. In addition, it establishes a work ethic in the district that the academic success of each individual student is important.

Strategy 31

Provide Practice to Master the Curriculum

Teachers and other instructional staff teach to individual student mastery of the objectives, providing ample practice opportunities over time for both short- and long-term mastery.

Strategy 31: WHAT

To maximize student achievement it is necessary to provide ample practice and learning opportunities for students to ensure both short- and long-term mastery of the material presented. Student achievement is increased when students have multiple experiences to gain speed and familiarity with the content, context, and cognitive requirements of the tested curriculum. Practice increases speed and familiarity. Speed and familiarity are elements impacting student-testing situations. The more familiar students are with the content and context of what's being tested, the greater the likelihood that the student will transfer learnings from the classroom to testing scenarios.

For practice to be effective, it must include short-term acquisition of skills, knowledge, and processes, and long-term mastery of the same. Students may not be tested over a given skill, knowledge, concept, or process for several months (or even years) after they first learned it. Take the case of students learning math concepts in the 1st, 2nd and 3rd grades but who aren't subjected to the state test until the end of the 4th grade. The skills, knowledge, and processes learned during those earlier school years will be part of that 4th

grade state test. It only makes sense for the educators of the system to provide intermittent reinforcement of the skills, knowledge, concepts, and processes these students will need to do well on the 4th grade test.

The old axiom "practice makes perfect" isn't quite explicit enough for our purposes here. What we are striving for with students is the statement, "perfect practice makes perfect." Practice schedules have to include assurance that the skills, knowledge, concepts, and processes students are practicing are the ones they will encounter on the district-designed or adopted tests and external assessments. Practice sessions must focus on the correct practice of skills, knowledge, concepts, or processes to ensure congruence with testing situations.

Strategy 31: WHY

"Perfect practice makes perfect!"

Practice is the way we learn. It is one of the main ways human beings learn anything–from playing a musical instrument to learning a skill or trade *(Zemelman, et al, 1998)*.[9] Most of the things we value in life are learned through repetitive practice. However, we provide students with precious little time for practice in those areas of academics where skill and knowledge acquisitions are crucial to tested performance. Student mastery of content and context is dependent upon practice. The ability of teachers to create practice sessions for students will determine to a great extent the degree of mastery attained. The higher the degree of mastery the better students will do on tested material. Therefore, the practice that students engage in *must be* congruent in content, context, and cognitive level with the material students will encounter on the test. If any of these three elements is missing, then the practice session will be out of alignment with tested material.

Remember, "Perfect practice makes perfect!"

Strategy Thirty-one–the HOW:

The following steps are suggested for establishing a system of student practice that will assist in providing for short-term acquisition and long-term mastery of skills, knowledge, and processes:

1. Define clearly the purpose of practice and communicate to instructional staff how practice helps develop long-term mastery.
2. Provide staff development for teachers on the appropriate use of practice and how to design and create meaningful practice sessions for students.

[9] Zemelman, Steven, Daniels, Harvey, and Hyde, Arthur (1998). *Best Practice, New Standards for Teaching and Learning in America's Schools*. Portsmouth, NH: Heinemann Publishers. p. 248.

3. Include the concept of practice in the staff development on monitoring for principals so they are able to assist teachers in appropriate practice session design and so they know the difference between effective and ineffective practice observed during classroom walk-throughs.
4. Have teachers map out their curriculum over a semester or a year showing how they will bring back initial student learnings into practice over time to move toward retention of the learning over time.
5. Design practice sessions into curriculum guides as an integral part of curriculum delivery. Make sure the focus of practice is congruent with the content, context, and cognitive levels of what students will encounter in test situations.
6. Emphasize the importance of "perfect practice makes perfect."

Speed of execution and familiarity with concepts and test formats are crucial for effective results on any state or norm-referenced test. It is classroom practice that increases speed and brings familiarity.

Strategy 32

Use Effective Teaching Practices

*Teachers have high engagement rates for all students
and use a variety of effective teaching practices*

Strategy 32: WHAT

Effective teachers use a variety of well-researched practices and methods to ensure student learning. They engage students in multiple-level learnings to ensure content acquisition and mastery as well as self-development, cognitive development, and metacognitive development. Effective teachers are aware that their specific behaviors and instructional strategies can alter student behavior and learning *(Marzano, 1998).*[10]

Effective teaching practices enable students to clearly understand what is expected from them for any given lesson. It also is structured to provide students with constructive feedback about their progress in attaining learning goals *(Hattie, 1992).*[11] One of the most powerful things effective teachers do is to set clear instructional goals and provide students with feedback on their success in meeting those instructional goals. Effective teachers are clear about the purpose and intended goal of their teaching and they design learning activities to elicit the specific behaviors and learnings they want from students. Effective

[10] Marzano, Robert J. (1998). "A Theory-Based Meta-Analysis of Research on Instruction." Mid-continent Regional Educational Laboratory: Aurora, Colorado.
[11] Hattie, J.A. (1992). *"Measuring the Effects of Schooling."* Australian Journal of Education, 36(1), 5-13.

teachers give each student in their classes many opportunities to respond to learning situations and know how to deal with student error in a manner that generates additional learning on the part of the individual and the entire class. They enhance the students' knowledge development, cognitive development, metacognitive development, and self-goals *(Marzano, 1998)*.[12]

Strategy 32: WHY

High-performing schools and school districts set high expectations for teachers. These expectations include the use of effective, researched teaching practices in the design and delivery of lessons in the classroom. Teacher knowledge and use of effective teaching strategies are a powerful determinant of student success. The instructional abilities of the teaching cadre within a school or district will help determine whether test scores rise, fall, or stay the same. Effective teaching practices will lead to higher student achievement.

Effective teaching practices engage a higher percentage of students in "on-task" behavior, produce higher student achievement, and increase student motivation and interest in the work they are doing in the classroom *(Bloom, 1999)*.[13]

Strategy 32: HOW

Effective teaching practices provide a critical key to improving student achievement. Specific instructional strategies and techniques must be devised for different instructional goals. Several instructional strategies have been shown to be effective regardless of the instructional goal. These instructional techniques include:

1. When presenting new knowledge or processes to students, provide them with advanced ways of thinking about the new knowledge or processes prior to presenting them.
2. When presenting students with new knowledge or processes, help them identify what they already know about the topic.
3. When students have been presented with new knowledge or processes, have them compare and contrast it with other knowledge and processes.
4. Help students represent new knowledge and processes in nonlinguistic ways as well as linguistic ways.

---

[12] Marzano, R.J., Ibid.

[13] Bloom, Benjamin S. (1999). *"The Search for Methods of Instruction."* Chapter in Ornstein, Allan C. and Behar-Horenstein, Linda S., et.al., *Contemporary Issues in Curriculum*. Needham Heights, MA: Allyn and Bacon.

5. Have students utilize what they have learned by engaging them in tasks that involve experimental inquiry, problem solving, and (presumably) decision-making and investigation.
6. Provide students with explicit instructional goals and give them explicit and precise feedback relative to how well those goals were met.
7. When students have met an instructional goal, praise and reward their accomplishments.
8. Have students identify their own instructional goals, develop strategies to obtain their goals and monitor their own progress.
9. When presenting new knowledge or processes, help students analyze the beliefs they have that will enhance or inhibit their chances of learning the new knowledge or processes *(Marzano, 1998)*."[14]

Develop and communicate high expectations for the use of effective teaching practices for all teachers in the system. Provide ongoing staff development to train teachers and administrators in the appropriate use of teaching practices. Make this staff development mandatory for all teachers and administrators. Provide ample opportunity for participants to practice their newly acquired skills. Provide opportunities for participants to see the effective teaching practices modeled with a variety of learning scenarios.

A good place to start this training is with the nine most powerful effective teaching practices as identified by Robert Marzono and others in the book *Classroom Instruction that Works, (Marzano, 1998).*[15]

Hold teachers accountable for the full use of effective teaching practices in their day-to-day lesson development. Hold building administrators accountable for monitoring effective teaching practices in their school. Central office administrators should be responsible for coaching and mentoring principals in their monitoring duties.

---

[14] Marzano, R.J., Ibid.
[15] Marzano, R.I. Ibid.

Strategy 33

Provide Students with Differentiated Time to Learn

Teachers and other instructional staff provide differentiated time for students to master the objectives, recognizing that students learn at different rates.

Strategy 33: WHAT

It has been said that "time is the coin of education." It is certainly one of the critical factors in the learning cycle for students. Education today is a time-based system. We expect students to learn everything we want them to learn within the time parameters we set for them. Obviously, some students need more time for learning than others. How a teacher accommodates the differences in learning time will go a long way toward mastery or nonmastery of the material being learned.

Each student has a unique learning rate. Teachers must be aware of these learning rates and make modifications in strategy and technique to adjust their teaching for the needs of students. The time required for each student to master the skills or concepts being presented is the time management standard for the teacher.

"If it is important enough to learn, it is important to provide the time needed to learn."

Strategy 33: WHY

Meeting the individual needs of students means adapting time and strategy or technique for each student. Perhaps more importantly, the *quality* of the time students spend overshadows the *quantity* of time spent. High-performing schools and school districts provide teachers with guidelines on the use of time for learning and acknowledge the decision-making responsibility of teachers to adjust, modify, and adapt their teaching to the individual needs of students. These schools and districts provide effective staff development for teachers and administrators on how to maximize learning within time constraints.

Short- and long-term mastery requires addressing the element of time. Providing quality time for learning challenges teachers to differentiate instruction based on the individual needs of students. High-performing school systems institutionalize differential use of learning time from the policy to the operational levels. It becomes part of the expectations of performance for teachers and administrators.

Strategy 33: HOW

The following steps are recommended to achieve this strategy:
1. First, establish a clear expectation relating to the use of instructional time. Teachers need to know what is expected of them and how the district defines differential instructional time.
2. Second, provide multiple opportunities for teachers (and administrators) to refine and hone their skills in using instructional time effectively. Modeling, on-the-job applications, and constructive feedback to teachers will enhance the quality of staff development in this area.
3. Next, train administrators to observe teachers' use of time as part of the monitoring of instruction. Administrator observations may provide data for the identification of topics or issues for site-based staff development.
4. Require teachers to monitor student academic learning time so that they have a sense of the learning rates of students in their class. Making notations about each student will provide the teacher with useful information in the design and delivery of instruction.

Adapting learning time to the needs of students increases the likelihood that students will master the essential skills, knowledge, and processes presented in the classroom. Acknowledging and acting upon differential learning time adds the ingredient that enables massive numbers of students to achieve mastery.

Strategy 34

Establish ILPs for Low-Achieving Students

Individual Learning Plans (ILPs) are developed for students who are underachieving, as indicated by test data. Low quartile students and/or "bubble" students are provided intensive assistance to remediate deficiencies.

Strategy 34: WHAT

An Instructional Learning Plan (ILP) is a specific intervention an effective school system uses to provide intensive assistance to low-achieving students. Low-achieving students are targeted to receive all the resources the school or district can bring to bear to prevent or remediate learning deficiencies. Individual learning plans are similar to plans created for special education students (IEPs-Individual Educational Plans). They are designed to focus instruction on those learnings identified as essential for students to become productive members of society and to perform well on district designed or adopted tests and external assessments. The ILP is a high-performing school's or district's way of providing a curriculum that will bring *all* students to high levels of learning.

An ILP is individualized for each student. It contains strategies, resources, assessments, and any other intervening factor deemed necessary to raise the academic achievement of the student. It focuses the activities of teachers and instructional support personnel as they work to eliminate student deficiencies.

Strategy 34: WHY

Schools and districts desiring to increase student achievement must target low-achieving students in order to get the greatest gains over time. Low-achieving students (especially those impacted by low socioeconomic status) require additional resources and time for learning. The ILP is designed to provide those resources and time. The implementation of the ILP maximizes the system's efforts to meet the individual needs of the student and increases the likelihood that the student will be prepared to respond to testing content and context. The ILP ensures that the instructional intervention is deeply aligned with the content, context, and cognitive levels of the test in use.

The ILP encourages focused, purposeful teaching. It guides lesson planning and gives the professional staff specific intervention strategies for each student. The teachers' ability to respond to the individual needs of the student is enhanced since the ILP provides the roadmap for success. The teacher manages, directs, and coaches the students to high levels of achievement. Using effective teaching practices, the power of teaching is multiplied exponentially. The ILP is the initial planning needed to differentiate the learning and the time for learning for each student (see Strategies 30 and 33).

Strategy 34: HOW

Schools and districts are well acquainted and skilled in developing Individualized Educational Plans (IEPs) for special education students. However, these skills have never been applied to non-special education students. The same skills and processes apply. The content and focus of the ILP is different from that of the IEP, but the intent is the same—provide each student with a plan of action to increase academic learning leading to mastery.

The following steps are suggested:
1. Identify and specify the individual learning needs of low-achieving students. Specify those needs in each of the major content areas. Include content and context deficiencies.
2. Identify and define instructional strategies for each content area. Design instructional lessons using effective teaching practices to ensure that instructional goals are met.
3. Include many opportunities for feedback to students on their progress in meeting instructional goals. Also include opportunities for students to assess their own progress and reflect on how they could improve their performance over time.
4. Ensure that all intervention strategies and techniques meet elements of deep alignment with the prescribed curriculum. Content, context, and cognitive levels

must be congruent with those of tested situations. A goal of the instructional intervention must be "no surprises" for students when they encounter tested items.

5. Develop, write, implement, check, revise (as necessary), and assess a plan to produce high levels of performance on assessments.

The ILP is the most effective way to impact achievement for low-performing students. It is instructionally sound and equitable. It offers the school or district a mechanism to increase learning for those students who need the most help.

ℭℜ *Analysis of Standard Four* ℰℴ

Now it is time for you to evaluate the status of your school or school district on *Standard Four: Use a Mastery Learning Approach and Effective Teaching Strategies.* For each strategy think about what the current status of your situation regarding these strategies and what changes need to be made. Write your responses in the space provided below.

STRATEGIES	CURRENT STATUS	CHANGES NEEDED
28. Implement a Mastery Learning Model	☐ Adequate ☐ Not adequate	
29. Align Teaching to the Curriculum	☐ Adequate ☐ Not adequate	
30. Provide Differentiated Instruction	☐ Adequate ☐ Not adequate	
31. Provide Practice to Master the Curriculum	☐ Adequate ☐ Not adequate	
32. Use Effective Teaching Practices	☐ Adequate ☐ Not adequate	
33. Provide Students with Differentiated Time to Learn	☐ Adequate ☐ Not adequate	
34. Establish ILPs for Low-Achieving Students	☐ Adequate ☐ Not adequate	

5

ॐ

STANDARD FIVE

Establish Curriculum Expectations, Monitoring, and Accountability

The following presents five highly powerful strategies regarding curriculum expectations, monitoring and accountability:

35. *State High Expectations for Achievement for Each Student*

36. *Monitor the Curriculum*

37. *Visit Classrooms and Provide Feedback*

38. *Use Disaggregated Data in the Decision-Making Process*

39. *Focus Staff Appraisal on Professional Growth*

Strategy 35

State High Expectations for Achievement for Each Student

The superintendent, senior officers, school-based administrators, and instructional staff articulate strong expectations for high student achievement for each student.

Strategy 35: WHAT

People of all ages are strongly motivated by high and reasonable expectations. This is particularly true for public school students. Because schools and school districts are systemic in nature, leadership for articulation of high expectations must start at the top or at least be institutionalized there. For example, strong Board of Education curriculum and instruction policy and philosophy statements clearly require that all school district employees should continuously articulate and demonstrate high expectations for each student's academic achievement and personal growth and development.

WHAT ARE THE WAYS WE CAN ESTABLISH HIGH EXPECTATIONS?

Strategy 35: WHY

First, numerous research studies, including the seminal study by Warner (1986), demonstrate that students experiencing higher expectations from their teachers achieve at higher levels than do students experiencing lower expectations from their teachers.

Second, years of organizational research and experience strongly show that the more successful organizations are those that have definitive philosophy statements and strong policies to direct their organizational operations. Since high expectations do affect learning, requirements for communicating expectations should appear in the manual.

Unfortunately, many schools today do not articulate strong achievement expectations to their students. This is frequently due to the fact that the link between achievement expectations and student achievement are not known or believed. It is also because requirements for such expectations are not included in school board policies or other district or school documents. Hence, principals, teachers, and other staff members are left to their own discretion to determine what, if any, expectations they should demonstrate for student achievement. We have interviewed school personnel who openly stated that they did not expect the students in their school or class to learn much. This is astounding. Their rationale was that their home environments, socioeconomic status, race, or other irrelevant factors prohibited students from doing so.

Strategy 35: HOW

The following steps are recommended for your consideration in establishing high expectations for student achievement in your school district:

1. Develop or revise a board policy and philosophy statement regarding high expectations for students in your school or school district. This could be part of an existing board or school curriculum and instruction policy.
2. Publish the new policy in the local newspaper and in all school district and school newsletters.
3. Include the requirements for high expectations in all school handbooks.
4. Train all central office and school staff (teachers, custodians, teacher aides) on the philosophy and research behind this policy.
5. Train all central office and school staff in techniques for articulating high and reasonable achievement expectations in a nurturing, caring, and firm manner.
6. Monitor staff to ensure that all staff are articulating high achievement expectations for all students to the community, parents, and students.
7. Provide further training and direction as needed to ensure that the board policy is being properly implemented.

Strategy 36

Monitor the Curriculum

Monitoring by district level officials, including the principals' supervisor, takes place regularly to determine the status of the school(s) and to coach the school-based administrators.

Strategy 36: WHAT

Monitoring of important functions is crucial to organizational effectiveness. The word "important" is operative here. School systems are so complex that not all functions can be monitored, but the more important functions must be monitored to ensure that the organization is on track in accomplishing its mission. For instance, Strategy 17 calls for the principal to ensure that all test data are disaggregated for the teachers' use and other purposes. This is a function that must be monitored since we know that teaching the information required on a test is crucial to student achievement.

There are two important facets of Strategy 36. First is the fact that important functions must be monitored to determine the organization's status quo in regard to each. Second is reflective coaching and goal setting. If the diagnosis determines that these functions are not being performed well, the supervisor and the school-based administrator must determine how to correct the situation. In cases where the school-based administrator is not performing adequately, a critical question for the supervisor to ask is if the person ever demonstrated the ability to perform the function. If so, then training is not likely to be the solution since the person already has the skill. If skill is lacking, then additional training may be an effective solution. If skill is not lacking, or if the person fails to respond adequately to the training, the problem may be an attitudinal one and the teacher may require extensive coaching or counseling. However, an often-overlooked problem is that other job demands are taking precedence over the main job function in question. This may be the fault of the district-level supervisor, someone higher up in the organization, or it may be a failure on the part of the employee to schedule time properly.

Another very important term for this Strategy is "monthly." Many district-level supervisors claim they simply do not have time to make monthly visits to the school sites. They often ask, why? But why would they *not* incorporate these visits as a high priority to coach and mentor principals and other school-based administrators in their work? This apathy indicates that training is strongly needed, that monthly visits may not be a high priority in an organization, or that central administration has overloaded the supervisor with too many duties of lesser importance.

Strategy 36: WHY

As a wise old saying goes, "If it is not monitored it is optional, and if it is optional it probably won't get done." When an organization has selected its mission and laid out its strategies for attaining it, the job duties inherent in those functions must be monitored to determine that they are being performed adequately. This aspect of monitoring may seem draconian or worth of Taylor, but it is not. All organizations that are successful over time monitor their progress and internal functions. When we speak of monitoring, we mean monitoring that is nurturing, supportive, mentoring, and coaching in nature.

Another very important aspect of monitoring is that of ensuring that the supervisor knows the status of important functions and any problems the supervisees may be confronting in completing the functions. As suggested earlier, a problem may be due to lack of training, job overload, or lack of definition of which functions are more important than others. After consultation with the supervisee, the supervisor must take action to correct the problem so that the supervisee can perform the job.

Strategy 36: HOW

The following steps are designed to help achieve this strategy and make it a successful practice in your school or school district:
1. Develop a strong policy statement about district-level managers monitoring at all levels in the organization to demonstrate the board's commitment to the practice.
2. Prioritize job duties of all central office supervisors to ensure that monitoring is a high priority.

3. Write monitoring requirements in all central office supervisors' job descriptions.
4. Provide training on monitoring of scheduling, supervisee's job requirements, student achievement, and reflective coaching to all central office supervisors.
5. Develop an evaluation strategy for assessing the effectiveness of monitoring practices.

Strategy 37

Visit Classrooms and Provide Feedback

Principals and/or other school-based administrators visit each classroom at least twice a week to monitor curriculum design, delivery alignment, quality of instruction, and classroom management and to provide feedback to staff for affecting higher student achievement.

Strategy 37: WHAT

Based on experience and research, it is believed that teachers are the most important element in the formal education of students. It follows that principals should be in classrooms. The classroom visits suggested here are not evaluative in nature; rather, they are facilitative. When in the classroom the principal should be observing to determine if the written curriculum is being delivered accurately, if students are learning objectives to mastery, if classroom management is proper and indicative of a high quality learning environment, if instructional strategies are being used properly, and if the teacher has the resources needed for effective teaching.

Following each visit, the principal should conduct a reflective feedback session with teachers observed, as appropriate. This session will provide valuable information to the principal and help clarify for the principal situations observed and not observed. Further, the session is used to provide feedback to the teacher. Many times teachers are so busy engaging in classroom activities that they are not aware of some of their behaviors and practices or they cannot observe important student behaviors. For instance, the principal may note that students in a certain area of the classroom are not engaged in the principle curriculum activity, are not called on by the teacher, or are misbehaving. These are valuable chunks of data for the teacher to use in redesigning instructional and classroom management strategies.

Another example might be of a teacher who is using a very effective strategy but who lacks the awareness of experience to know when it is best to use the strategy. Coaching feedback could be just what the teacher needs to effectively utilize the technique in question.

Strategy 37: WHY

Numerous research studies show that school principal visits to the classroom are strongly linked to important outcomes, including improved student achievement. Ten important outcomes and the related research studies are referenced below.

1. **Improved teacher self-efficacy** (Frase, 2001; Chester and Beaudin, 1996)
2. **Improved teacher attitudes toward professional development** (Frase, 2001)
3. **Improved teacher attitudes toward teacher appraisal** (Frase, 2001 and 1998)
4. **Improved teacher satisfaction as define as "flow" Experiences** (Frase, 2001)
5. **Increase perceived teacher efficacy of other teacher** (Frase, 1998 and 2001) **and of the school** (Frase, 2001)
6. **Improved classroom instruction** (Teddlie, Kirby, and Springfield, 1989)
7. **Improved teacher perceived effectiveness of the school** (Frase 1998 and 2001)
8. **Improved teacher perception of principal effectiveness** (Frase, Andrews and Soder, 1987; Blasé, 1991; Heck, et al, 1990; Mortimer, 1989; Sago, 1992; Valentine, 1981; and Wimpelberg, et al, 1989)
9. **Improved student discipline and student acceptance of advice and criticism** (Blase's 1987 and 1991)
10. **Higher Student Achievement Across Cultural Lines and SES Levels** (Andrews, Soder and Jacoby, 1986; Andrews, R. and Soder, R., 1987; Heck, 1991; Heck, 1992; Louis and Miles, 1991; Hallinger and Heck, 1995)

Actual practices of principals are frequently in accordance with these findings. Numerous studies show that principals spend more time in meetings, in their offices, on playgrounds, and even off campus than in classrooms.

The "Why" of classroom visits is quite clear when we consider these research findings. But there is also empirical and practical evidence to support the benefit of principals being in classrooms. Many of the authors of this book were also superintendents and principals. As practicing administrators we saw the effect of frequent, well-focused classroom visits. As is frequently the case in the social sciences, research has finally caught up with practice.

Strategy 37: HOW

The following guidelines are offered for implementing this strategy:

1. Include the philosophy and directive for frequent and well-focused classroom visits in board policy—preferably in both management and curriculum policies.
2. Include the requirement for classroom visits in the principals' job descriptions.
3. Include monitoring of classroom visits in the principals' supervisors' job descriptions.
4. Provide extensive training in high-quality instruction, the relationship (alignment) between instruction and the written curriculum, techniques for assessing the alignment between the taught and written curriculum, and effective methods of reflective coaching.
5. Monitor the frequency and results of classroom visits in the monthly monitoring as described in Strategy 36.
6. Develop and implement an evaluation strategy to determine the effectiveness and impact of principal classroom visits.

Strategy 38

Use Disaggregated Data in the Decision-Making Process

Principal ensures that all test data are appropriately disaggregated for teachers and used in decision-making.

Strategy 38: WHAT

The first aspect of this strategy deals with test data disaggregation at the district, school, classroom, and student levels. Disaggregation means that the test items are isolated (identified) by skill through deconstruction and linked to curriculum objectives based on content. In the past, test data disaggregation had to be performed by school personnel, typically the principal. Today, however, most test manufacturers perform test data disaggregation for a fee. This is a service the principal or central office administration should order when the specifications for the test data returns are communicated to the testing company. When test companies or central office personnel do not perform this function, the principal must.

Linking the results with the district/school curriculum objectives is absolutely crucial in order to best inform curriculum decision-making. This task should be accomplished by district personnel, the principal, or other school personnel, and is much easier when the district's written curriculum and taught curriculum are well aligned with the tested curriculum-in other words, when the curriculum is backloaded.

Levels of Test Data Disaggregation

School level: At this level, the principal disaggregates the test data to indicate how the school, the grade levels, grade level clusters (e.g., grades 1-3/4-6) and special programs are performing on specific objectives, clusters of objectives, and total subject areas. The key here is that the disaggregated data should be used to inform instruction and curriculum emphasis. That is, if students in a certain grade or program are not meeting the expected performance levels on a certain cluster of objectives or a total subject area, then changes in curriculum emphasis and instruction are needed. The changes are directed by the data derived from the disaggregated test data.

Classroom Level: At the classroom level, the teacher is interested in knowing how well his or her class and individual students performed on each subject area, subsection, cluster of objectives, and individual objective. The disaggregated data should be used by teachers to make changes in their programs so that each student has a better opportunity to perform well on the next test.

This is a brief overview of test result disaggregation. It is the principal's responsibility to ensure that refined, disaggregated data is available at the school, grade, classroom, and special program levels for each area tested.

The second section of Strategy 38 involves ensuring that the disaggregated data are used to influence curriculum and instruction. Disaggregated data, just as raw test data, have no legitimate value unless they are used to inform curriculum and instructional decision-making. Ensuring use is one of the principal's monitoring functions. Monitoring can be accomplished by including this topic in grade level and faculty meetings where test results and plans for using the data are discussed, by conducting individual and group interviews with teachers to discuss their individual programs and teaching changes for groups and individual students, and by making frequent visits to classrooms (see Strategy 37). The objective is to ensure that the disaggregated data are used to inform curriculum and instruction decision-making to improve student achievement.

Strategy 38: WHY

A major complaint about standardized testing by its naysayers is that the results are used for undesirable political propaganda and that they do not inform decision-making in schools. The first issue is largely out of our control since newspaper writers and politicians are responsible, but the second issue is fully within the control of the public schools. Another complaint is that the tests do not measure all or even the most important information and skills students must acquire. We agree, but what test does? We know of none. Further, we have not observed information addressed on a standardized test that does not seem important for students to learn. Based on this reasoning and the fact that we do not have the option of administering or not administering the tests, and the fact that the test results will be used to judge the success of public schooling, we believe that public school administrators must use test results to ensure high student achievement.

There is another, broader reason for the public school to produce high test scores. Public confidence in the schools is at a very low ebb, and to turn the tide we must demonstrate that we can do the job. After all, public schools and the people who work in them do so at the will of the legislature and the public. Some public school personnel and university professors adamantly denounce the use of standardized tests and advocate for other forms of assessment. We believe that they may be right, but we will not have the opportunity to demonstrate the value of alternate forms of assessment unless we demonstrate we can do the job on standardized tests.

Strategy 38: HOW

Try the following steps to achieve this strategy:

1. First, determine if the test results have been disaggregated. If so, acquire it. If not, conduct the disaggregation by analyzing (deconstructing) each item to determine the objective it measures. For further information regarding deconstruction see the "How" section of Strategy 1.
2. Match the objectives tested by the standardized test (item by item) and match each to the appropriate objective in your curriculum.
3. Create a list of the test objectives that were and were not achieved. This should be done at the school, program, grade, classroom, and individual student levels.
4. Identify those objectives that were not adequately achieved and those that may be over-taught, and make curriculum delivery (instruction) changes as needed. The areas not being adequately addressed may vary from subject area to subject area, skill cluster to skill cluster, classroom-to-classroom, or student-to-student. Lists of all data should be developed.
5. Prepare teachers for receiving these data by informing them of the purpose of disaggregating data and its use in redesigning* curriculum and instruction.
6. Schedule and conduct faculty, grade level, or other meetings for distributing the data, analyzing it, and making decisions to improve curriculum design and delivery.
7. Monitor the use of disaggregated data by:
   - Making it a topic of discussion at each faculty and grade level meeting.
   - Frequently visiting classrooms to observe the conduct of planned changes in curriculum delivery (instruction).

- Reviewing weekly and monthly test results.
8. Discuss your school's test scores and the curriculum delivery changes made to improve achievement with other principals and central office administrators, and present related information to the parents and community.
9. Develop and display graphs, charts, or other graphics that clearly communicate objectives targeted and students' attainment of objectives over time.

*Note: Curriculum design is a central district function, however, the school principal may see that objectives being tested by certain test items are not included in the written curriculum. In this case, the principal should inform central office officials. If they do not respond or respond too slowly in making curriculum changes, we recommend that prudent changes be made at the school level to ensure that students have a fair opportunity to learn to material they will be tested on.

Strategy 39

Focus Staff Appraisal on Professional Growth

The staff appraisal/evaluation process focuses on the professional growth of staff in the accomplishment of high student achievement.

Strategy 39: WHAT

The purpose of teacher and principal appraisals should be to improve instruction so that student learning is maximized. To this end, every state legislature has enacted laws requiring yearly or biyearly appraisals of teachers and administrators. Unfortunately, numerous studies have shown that teacher and principal evaluations have either not been performed or were performed with the intent to satisfy only, that is, to meet the minimal requirements of the law but not to improve instruction. In fact, numerous surveys show that teachers and principals resoundingly say that their evaluations are a waste of time—they say that evaluations do not help them improve their instruction, the original and sole purpose.

The reasoning for the laws is clear—teachers are the most important element in the formal education of a student. In order to do the best job possible in providing an education, teachers must be well trained in their craft. Staff appraisal is one means of diagnosing teachers' instructional strengths and weaknesses. Note that the operative word here is "instructional." We find that many times teachers and administrators are appraised on the basis of non-classroom or non-instructional criteria such as committee membership, evening meeting attendance and the like. These are important, but far less so than teaching.

The results of appraisals should be used as the basis for developing and carrying out a professional development plan for each teacher and administrator. The subsequent appraisal, specified classroom visits, and conferences with the teacher should serve as follow-ups to assess the effect of the professional development activities.

Some school personnel and professors contend that instruction cannot be linked to student achievement as indicated by test results. We disagree. A very strong research base exists on which instructional practices yield high student learning. This information must be used to inform teachers and administrators as they attempt to improve student achievement. That is the purpose of professional development.

Strategy 39: WHY

The first and primary rationale for Strategy 39 is that student achievement, or learning, is the intended product of the public schools. Today state legislatures have defined learning as that which standardized tests measure. It is our job as public school administrators to produce learning. The second rational for the strategy is that teachers are assigned the responsibilities of designing high quality instruction in order to effectively deliver curriculum to students. Their success in doing so is greatly determined by their instructional skills.

Simple as that! The public schools are in the business of producing learning and the best way to accomplish that is high-quality instruction. This statement has its naysayers. Some people, including some teachers and administrators, believe that schools cannot overcome the impact of home life and socioeconomic status. They say that the large majority of children from low-income families simply cannot do well on tests and certainly will not learn at nearly the same level as higher income students. The reality is that they are wrong. Numerous studies and experiences by school districts clearly show that high-quality curriculum design (deep alignment between the written, taught, and tested curriculum) and high-quality teaching can result in helping low-income and poverty-stricken children achieve high test scores. To think otherwise is losing cause for hope and sight of purpose. If the public schools, as an institution, cannot produce learning for children from all socioeconomic status levels, they will be put out of business.

Administrators' appraisals, too, should focus on professional growth to improve student achievement. Principals are given the responsibility to ensure that all students in their schools learn. Their appraisals should be based on their ability to analyze and diagnose curriculum and instruction, to cooperatively develop and monitor teacher professional growth plans, and to attain targeted learning levels as measured by the given test or assessment procedure.

Strategy 39: HOW

Try these activities for accomplishing this strategy:

1. Review the last few teacher or principal evaluations you performed. How closely focused were they on curriculum design and delivery? Give the teachers an anonymous survey asking for frank comments on the worth of the appraisal process in helping them improve student achievement. Make changes in the practice as necessary.

2. Inform teachers that instructional improvement is the goal of the teachers, the principal, and administrators at all levels. Further, inform them that everyone can improve, and seeking improvement is healthy, not a sign of failure. We know of no perfect person.

3. Establish high-quality instruction and high student achievement as the number one goal for your school/district. Try these ideas to instill the philosophy:

    • Make improved student achievement and instruction the primary purpose of all faculty meetings, training events, grade level meetings, and individual meetings with staff.

    • Arrange for teachers to observe other teachers teaching and to share their observations.

    • Arrange for teachers to observe the principal teach and to give constructive feedback.

4. Focus teacher appraisals on instruction with the goal of improving student achievement.

5. Seek frequent teacher input on the effectiveness of the appraisal system on improving curriculum design, instruction, and student achievement as appropriate for the teacher's position.

6. Design the appraisal process around a professional growth plan.

⊙ℛ *Analysis of Standard Five* ℰ𝒪

Now it is time for you to evaluate the status of your school or school district on *Standard Five: Establish Curriculum Expectations, Monitoring, and Accountability*. For each strategy think about the current status of your situation and the changes you feel are needed. Write your responses in the spaces provided.

STRATEGY	CURRENT STATUS	CHANGES NEEDED
35. State High Expectations for Achievement for Each Student	❏ Adequate ❏ Not adequate	
36. Monitor the Curriculum	❏ Adequate ❏ Not adequate	
37. Visit Classrooms and Provide Feedback	❏ Adequate ❏ Not adequate	
38. Use Disaggregated Data in the Decision-Making Process	❏ Adequate ❏ Not adequate	
39. Focus Staff Appraisal on Professional Growth	❏ Adequate ❏ Not adequate	

6

STANDARD SIX

Institute Effective District and School Planning, Staff Development and Resource Allocation, and Provide a Quality Learning Environment

The following presents eleven highly powerful strategies regarding planning, staff development, use of resources, and the learning environment itself:

40. *Create and Implement a Singular, Focused, Multiyear District Plan Incorporating Change Strategies for Higher Student Achievement*

41. *Align School Plans to the District Plan*

42. *Meet the CMSi Plan Design Criteria*

43. *Implement Aligned Teacher Training to Reach District and School Goals*

44. *Implement Administrative Training Aligned to the Curriculum, and Its Assessment and District Plan Priorities*

45. *Provide Differentiated Staff Development*

46. *Link Resource Allocations to Goals, Objectives, Priorities, and Diagnosed Needs of the System*

47. *Provide Qualified and Adequate Personnel*

48. *Remove Incompetent Staff*

49. *Provide a Quality Learning Environment*

50. *Provide Quality Facilities*

Strategy 40

Create and Implement a Singular-Focused, Multiyear District Plan Incorporating Change Strategies for Higher Student Achievement

Planning is built into one comprehensive district improvement plan that consolidates all planning efforts. The plan focuses on two or three academic goals for multiyear periods of time. The plan incorporates effective change strategies including professional development endeavors.

Strategy 40: WHAT

Organizational planning is more than simply deciding what you are going to do next week. High-quality planning must be long-range and incorporate numerous considerations and elements to ensure that the results are as accurate as possible. Successful businesses and school districts know precisely what they want to accomplish for their clients and how they are going to satisfy those client needs. There are many definitions and models of planning and all have strengths and weaknesses. The Curriculum Management Improvement Model (developed and recommended by CMSi) specifies thirteen components required for high-quality, long-range planning. These are described in Strategy 42.

Planning needs to be focused and well thought-out. We see many school districts engaging in planning, but most have far too many goals, and strategic actions are separate and isolated from other actions. Large groups of people come together, often in forums, to identify the goals. A collective approach is used and many goals are established well beyond the capacity of the district to carry them out. It is time to stop this type of planning.

Many governing boards and administrators fail to clearly distinguish between board goals and management goals. Board goals should be mission-oriented and focused on results—student achievement goals. Management goals need to focus on the means for accomplishing the results goals. It is our opinion that the direction of the management goals needs to be tightly held in low-performing districts with a focus on just two or three management goals for intense intervention to accomplish higher student achievement.

Although many districts have plans, most do not get implemented. Just making the plan and carrying it out in a perfunctory manner seems to be the goal for many-simply to meet a requirement-rather than having it actually serve as a blueprint for change. Moreover, the strategic actions frequently identified have little chance of bringing about higher student achievement. The strategies are often not well researched and change approaches are not incorporated. The research is replete with change strategies, but often these are ignored.

Strategy 40: WHY

Lewis Carroll provided us with the finest of all rationales for planning. In his famous book *Through the Looking Glass* he described the confusion of the book's main character, Alice, walking down a road. She came to a fork in the road and did not know which fork to follow. She spied the wise Cheshire cat in the tree and queried, "Which path should I take?" The wise cat responded, "Where is it you wish to go?" She responded, "I don't know." At that the Cheshire cat exclaimed, "Then either will do fine." So much truth and wisdom is contained in this brief conversation. If we do not know where we want to go, then any path or activity will do fine and any destination will be acceptable. But school districts cannot take just any road. Today, vouchers and charter schools challenge the public school monopoly and much proposed legislation offers more serious threats. Public schools must deliver the goods as defined by the external clients-parents, the public, and the state legislatures-or the arena of competition will be opened up and public education will lose a major part of its market share. Organizations that do the best job meeting the needs expressed by the public will stay in existence and thrive. Doing so implicitly means defining and maintaining a clear and narrow focus and strategically planning a means for attaining the goals of ever higher student achievement.

For schools this means focusing on two or three academic goals to be attained over a one- to three-year period of time. Individual schools must follow school district missions, but in doing so they must be certain that their students learn the basics as defined by the legislature and the school district. Gone are the days when superintendents and school principals could satisfy the community and parents by telling them that the school was teaching highly valuable skills and talents indiscernible by objective or empirical measures.

It is foolhardy to believe that people can accomplish a complicated task that they do not have the skills to achieve. Hence, long-range planning must also include those who are designated to deliver the specified products. The CMSi rationale for long-range planning is straightforward in its belief that teachers are the primary deliverers of learning to students. Therefore, a long-range plan must include the professional development needs of teachers simply because they (teachers) do the most valuable job in any school district—directly impacting student achievement. Those who supervise them, the school principals, also can impact their success in large part. Principals are responsible for monitoring the school curriculum and the quality of the curriculum delivery demonstrated by teachers. Research (Frase, Heck, etc.) has shown that student achievement in schools where principals actively monitor classroom instruction is higher than in other schools, and the teachers demonstrate higher respect for principals, profess higher perceived efficacy for other teachers and the administration, and hold teacher evaluation and staff development in higher regard.

Planning at the local school level must be systematic and result in specific targets and goals. Without specifying these, the school cannot know the learning, skills, attitudes, or values it wishes to deliver to its students; otherwise, activities, although well intended, will be wasted.

Strategy 40: HOW

The following steps are recommended for making Strategy 40an essential characteristic of your school:

1. Determine the district's overall mission, vision, and long-range plan.
2. Establish clear student achievement goals and have these approved by the board as their board goals.
3. Establish multiyear management goals, few in number, that have a high probability of impacting student achievement. Strategies must be researched and data-driven in selection.
4. Use the criteria shared in Strategy 42 to develop the district plan and keep planning streamlined and integrated.

5. Ensure that the results of planning–the goals, objectives, and action plans–are doable.
6. Carry out the plan and monitor it, not letting day-to-day operations move you from the aim of the plan.

Strategy 41

Align School Plans to the District Plan

*The school plan is aligned to a focused, district-wide
plan for increased student achievement.*

Strategy 41: WHAT

This book is about what needs to be in place for school staff to raise student achievement. It is important to remember that schools do not exist in a vacuum. As per Curriculum Management Systems, Inc. (CMSi), the unit of analysis of a curriculum management audit is the school district, and even though this book focuses on each individual schools' staff, we must be aware that the individual school is part of a community and a larger system know as a school district. School districts are systemic in nature and, as such, all subsystems within them must work together to attain a common mission or product. That product, per CMSi, is learning, however your state legislature and local school board choose to define it. This projected product is what gives schools their direction, and each school within the system must establish plans to attain the district product.

Strategy 41: WHY

The key words regarding the rationale, or the "why" of this strategy, are "alignment" and "congruency." In Strategy 1 you learned that district content standards, and thus, the school content standards must be aligned with state standards. In Strategy 2 you learned that objectives must be clear and precise and aligned to the content standards in order to communicate exactly what is to be learned. Strategy 3 was about aligning objectives with external assessments to ensure congruency of objectives with the external assessment. Strategy 19 focused on ensuring that all programs in a school are aligned to the district objectives. Strategy 25 says that all instructional resources must be purchased based on their alignment to the objectives and used accordingly. Finally, Strategies 26 through 34 were about aligning teaching practices to deliver the objectives while considering differing student needs.

So what was the purpose of reviewing these strategies? That's a good question whose answer is crucial: all of these strategies lay the groundwork for district-wide planning and the need for schools to derive their plan from the district plan, *in order to insure alignment*. If a school chooses to go its own way, there can be no assurance that the students will achieve common goals that the district or state has deemed most important. Following the district plan is the first step in ensuring that the school plan is congruent with or aligned to the district plan. Public schools are not in private practice. They are part of a system and, as such, must devote themselves to the district's direction.

An unfortunate fact is that many school districts do not have a long-range plan. While conducting well over 300 audits, we have been distressed to learn this fact. What does this mean to school staff should your district not have a long-range plan? Very simply, it means that you must do it yourself.

Strategy 41: HOW

1. Obtain a copy of the district long-range plan.
2. Read the mission statement and determine how goals and objectives and action plans are linked, or are aligned to, the mission statement.
3. The next step is to begin development of your school mission statement. In this step be sure to consider vital data about all facets of your school (internal environment) and the community (external) environments. What does the near future hold for them regarding enrollment changes, evolving curriculum needs, etc.? In the curriculum management audit, we call this "critical analysis" and "assumptions."

4. Develop your school mission statement in cooperation with teachers, parents, and possibly other community representatives.

5. Seek to gain commitment to the plan from these participants.

6. Ensure that the mission statement communicates a definite direction and is not so broad as to be meaningless. Remember, the mission statement defines what your school is all about (see Strategy 42).

7. Communicate this mission widely so that all groups within your school community know what the mission is and understand it.

8. From the mission statement, develop a few goals in alignment to district goals. Each goal should contribute to the attainment of the mission statement. If you have multiple goals that are focused in a given direction, group these goals as components.

9. Develop specific, measurable objectives for each goal. The objectives should state who will do what, when, how, and how success will be determined. Remember, objectives must be very clear so that those assigned the job of achieving them know exactly what to do and exactly how their success will be determined.

10. For each objective or group of objectives, develop action plans designed to deliver the objectives and, ultimately, the goals and mission statement.

11. Develop this plan for use over a three-year period.

12. Develop a sub plan for each year of the three years.

13. Throughout this process, ensure that your plan is congruent with the district plan, and last, but not least, be sure you have not bitten off too much. Is your plan doable given human resource and budget considerations? All activities must be linked and integrated into the budget to ensure proper funding: 1-9.

14. If the district does not have a long-range plan, suggest that they need to develop one; then, if necessary, develop on yourself at the school level.

Strategy 42

Meet CMSi Plan Design Criteria

The district and school plans meet the CMSi plan design criteria.

Strategy 42: WHAT

Curriculum Management Systems, Inc., (CMSi) has developed the Curriculum Management Improvement Model which includes thirteen criteria for assessing the quality of a long-range plan. They are listed in *Figure 21*.

Figure 21

Curriculum Management Audit Criteria for Assessing System Long-Range Planning
Setting Direction
1. ***Mission:*** General-purpose benefits and educational goals of a school organization. The mission provides a description of expectations and system requirements relative to identification of the primary client, intended results, general approaches, and personnel to carry out the mission. The mission is the foundation upon which *all* educational programs and services are built. It describes the reason a district exists. Highly successful organizations (both public and private) usually have a clearly defined and communicated mission expressed in planning documents.

2.	**_Critical Analysis:_** Collection and analysis of vital data about all facets of the internal and external environments of the school organization. It defines the status of a school organization and describes its future by combining forecasting results with status-check results.
3.	**_Assumptions:_** A prediction of the events and conditions that are likely to influence the performance of a school organization, division, or key individuals. Preparing planning assumptions is a form of forecasting. Assumptions are concerned with what the organization's future will look like, and they help bridge the gap between needs and actions in the planning process.
4.	**_Components:_** Means of grouping goals for the purpose of communicating and management. All goals will be assigned to a component and each component will consist of one or more goals.
5.	**_Objectives:_** Statements of results that are measurable and have time limitations. They describe the condition(s) a school organization wants to improve. The desired improvements are then translated into goals. Objectives are written for each goal. As objectives are met, goals are accomplished.
6.	**_Evaluation:_** Statements of conditions that show evidence that an objective is satisfactorily achieved and procedures developed for completing the evaluation. Each objective should be evaluated and the evaluation procedures should be developed at the time the objective is written.

Deploying Direction

7.	**_Action Plans:_** Actions to be taken that will help achieve the objectives. Each objective will have one or more activities. Significant elements of each activity include a due date, responsible person(s), and costs.
8.	**_Plan(s) Integration:_** Each unit manager's plan is integrated into the budget for consideration. There is integration of plans with respect to the mission and resources. Feasibility with budget is determined and plans are checked against the organizational beliefs and mission statement.
9.	**_Planning and Budget Timeline Relationships_**: Goals and action plans are in place and integrated prior to the budgeting process.
10.	**_Multiyear Planning and Goal Integration:_** Planning extends over several years, and the number of goals and actions are feasible within the resources of the district.
11.	**_Linkage Documents:_** All documents in a system, particularly school plans, are aligned to the district plan.

Managing Direction
12. *Stakeholders Commitment:* All stakeholders in a system (community, board, administrators, staff, and students) are represented in development of the plan.
13. *Plan Design Monitoring:* System for assessing the status of activities, analyzing the results, and reporting outcomes are built into the design of the plan.

Strategy 42: WHY

Mediocrity is so easy that no planning is required. But we know of no teacher or principal who wants to be known for mediocrity. Instead, all want to be high achievers. History has shown, and it is the belief of CMSi, that only those organizations, schools, and people who plan and define their destination attain high levels of success. In today's ever-changing world, future planning is not an option, it's a requirement. Based on the wide experience of CMSi, the thirteen criteria provided above define high quality, long-range planning.

Strategy 42: HOW

Refer to the "How" section in *Strategy 41*. Throughout this section link your activities to the fourteen criteria. To help, the steps in *Strategy 41* are provided below. Each is keyed to the respective criterion or criteria provided in *Figure 21*.

1. Obtain a copy of the district long-range plan (1& total plan).
2. Read the mission statement and determine how goals and objectives and action plans are linked, or are aligned to, the mission statement (1, 4, 5, & 7).
3. The next step is to begin development of your school mission statement. In this step be sure to consider vital data about all facets of your school (internal environment) and the community (external) environments. What does the near future hold for them regarding enrollments changes, evolving curriculum needs, etc? In the curriculum management audit, we call this "critical analysis" and "assumptions" (2 & 3).
4. Develop your school mission statement, regardless of whether your district has a mission statement or long-range plan, in cooperation with teachers, parents, and possibly other community representatives (1 & 12).
5. Seek to gain commitment to the plan from these participants (12).
6. Ensure that the mission statement communicates a definite direction and is not so broad it is meaningless. Remember, the mission statement defines what your school is all about (see *Strategy 42*) (1).

7. Communicate this mission widely so that all groups within your school community know what the mission is and understand it (12).

8. From the mission statement, develop goals that are in alignment to district goals. Each goal should contribute to the attainment of the mission statement. If you have multiple goals that focus in a given direction, group these goals as components (4).

9. Develop specific measurable objectives for each goal. The objectives should state who will do what, when, and how, and how success will be determined. Remember, objectives must be very clear so that those assigned the job of achieving them know exactly what to do and exactly how their success will be determined (5 & 6).

10. For each objective or group of objectives, develop action plans designed to deliver the objectives and, ultimately, the goals and mission statement (7).

11. Develop this plan for use over a three-year period (10).

12. Develop a sub-plan for each year of the three years (10).

13. Throughout this process, ensure that your plan is congruent with the district plan, and last, but not least, be sure you have not bitten off more that you can chew. That is, are your plans doable within the human resource and budget considerations within which you must operate? All activities must be linked and integrated into the budget to ensure proper funding (1 & 9).

14. If the district does not have a long-range plan, suggest that they need to develop one; then, if necessary, develop one yourself at the school level.

Strategy 43

Implement Aligned Teacher Training To Reach District and School Goals

Teachers receive and participate in ongoing training as part of reaching the goals in the district and school improvement plans.

Strategy 43: WHAT

Teachers are the prime deliverers of the mission of the school system. They are the "firing line" officers charged with the primary responsibility to deliver the learning specified by the system. Teachers need to receive and participate in ongoing training as part of reaching the system's goals and of achieving the school's improvement plan. Teachers are the most important group in the organization in terms of the organization accomplishing its goals.

Without training aligned with the system's goals and improvement plans, teachers have little or no direction on the procedural steps to take or the processes to implement in order to reach those goals. Where there is no understanding of goals or plans there is a "rudderless" administration, and it is impossible to predict the system's final destination. Training needs to be relevant, based on solid data regarding organizational performance, and focused on building competence, commitment, and effectiveness in confronting and overcoming organizational obstacles to reaching the system's mission and goals.

Strategy 43: WHY

Curriculum audits have often found that teacher training is unfocused and voluntary in its design and delivery. The connection between organizational aims and purposes is often weak, or in some cases, nonexistent. Rational organizations define and develop aims and purposes, design and implement action to achieve those purposes, and monitor performance for informed decision-making relative to progress and corrective action.

Once the system focuses its energies on specific goals, goals selected and determined by research-based information that documents real need, the system must initiate the process of optimization. Optimizing an organization requires keeping an "eye on the ball" and preventing fragmentation or distraction from the goal. It also calls for aligning all activities and resources of the organization with its purposes. Planning is simply a design and schedule of actions to be taken to satisfy and fulfill organizational needs (identified as discrepancies between what the system wants to accomplish and what it has accomplished currently).

Key personnel are the human resources that give the organization the means to satisfy needs, meet goals, and accomplish organizational aims and purposes. It goes without question that key personnel must be included in training activities designed to prepare, reinforce, and shape behaviors congruent with the system's goals and purposes. Of course, this means teachers. If the product of the school system is learning, the teacher is the builder of that product. To build it in accordance with organizational intentions, training is needed that matches what the system intends to accomplish.

Strategy 43: HOW

Training needs to be goal-focused, needs-driven, compatible with best practice, and adequate in scope and quality. To accomplish these attributes, consider the following steps and actions:

1. Clarify and document the organizational aims, purposes, objectives, and mission. There is nothing more damaging to organizational effectiveness than confusion about what the system stands for, believes in, and is trying to accomplish. Training needs to be designed to develop comprehensive understanding of the organization's direction among teachers and to build fidelity and loyalty to the organization's mission. It is critical that personnel in the system acknowledge and

internalize that individuals within an organization must support the organization's aims and purposes if the organization is to endure.

2. Conduct a needs assessment of how well the system is achieving its aims and purposes. This step is akin to "taking stock" to see where the organization is compared to its desired status. This assessment of standing and performance must be clearly connected to the system's expectations, goals, and purpose. The data gathered should inform teachers and others in training conferences of where the system is falling short, where it is reaching its goals, and where the system is exceeding its goals. Training needs to be designed to acquaint teachers with where the system is in terms of effectiveness and success.

3. Develop options and alternatives to address organizational needs. Once training has been completed as to what the organization wants to accomplish and how well it is doing against those intentions, teachers need to participate in training activities designed to develop and to visualize meeting identified needs. Training needs to be provided in topics related to research findings, peer organization experience, theoretical approaches, documented "best practice," etc. At this point, the organization needs to decide which courses of action it will follow.

4. Train teachers in the procedures and processes needed to complete the courses of action selected. It is not enough to identify and adopt a plan to implement a promising organizational strategy. Teachers need to be trained in the following:
   - The course of action
   - How it works
   - What it takes to make it work
   - How to support it
   - How to determine if it's working satisfactorily

5. Don't overlook the necessity of dissemination of results and progress. Teachers need to be trained to solve organizational problems, but once trained, they need feedback on progress and performance to aid in operational decision-making. Operational decisions may include continuation of strategies, modification of strategies, or termination of strategies. Without training and feedback, uninterrupted progress is impossible.

6. Educational leaders need to be aware of the power and necessity of appropriate training. Given adequate and relevant training, teachers can focus their pedagogy and energy on accomplishing the goals and mission of the system.

Strategy 44

Implement Administrative Training Aligned to the Curriculum, Its Assessment, and District Plan Priorities

The principal and other school-based administrators receive and participate in ongoing training directly related to curriculum design and delivery, curriculum monitoring, student and curriculum assessment and district and school improvement plan implementation.

Strategy 44: WHAT

Administrators can make or break good school systems. The leader is the most critical person in the organization, and has the strongest influence on the internal integrity and character of the organization. Without leadership skills, management savvy, and curriculum knowledge, the leader is impeded in building organizational effectiveness and success in the design and delivery of learning.

Training can make a huge difference in the skills, capabilities, and knowledge of school administrators, particularly in curriculum management. The role of the leader in curriculum management is critical to the success of the system in reaching its goals and objectives for learners. Without adequate and valuable training, the organization will not to accomplish its aims and purposes.

Strategy 44: WHY

Curriculum management consists of several discrete and unique factors that must be constructed and implemented successfully, and they must be crafted and woven together in a system that is functional, practicable, and sound. Administrative personnel must provide the leadership to put all of the components of a sound curriculum management system in place and to develop the relationships necessary for the components to work in concert.

The school system would find it very difficult to be successful in achieving its goals and purposes without strong administrative leadership. Administrative leadership would find it very difficult to be successful in leading the organization without suitable and pertinent training. Training is the glue that pulls the components together and makes them work harmoniously toward achieving the goals and purposes of the organization.

Strategy Forty-four–the HOW:

Follow these steps to implement this strategy:

1. Identify relevant knowledge for principals and school administrators in curriculum management and provide training regarding-
   - Board policies and system expectations for schools, employees, and learners
   - System curriculum objectives (what students are to know, think, do, feel, or be like) as authorized by the governing authority.
   - State, national, content area standards or testing components.
   - System job descriptions for educational leaders (knowledge, skills, communication, modeling, duties and responsibilities).

2. Diagnose school leaders' strengths and weaknesses in critical curriculum management skills. Include curriculum design and delivery, instructional efficacy, effectiveness in working with people, and data management requirements (key data on status, progress, growth, change, etc. of measured learning).

3. Design and develop training to fill in the gaps of administrator knowledge, skills, and behaviors in curriculum management. Train administrators in the need for direction–i.e., "What the curriculum *is* and how to know if it is valid." Other attributes of curriculum management to be included in administrator training are:
   - The nature and power of curriculum quality control.
   - Defined specific learner objectives that are expected to be attained.
   - Scope and quality of curriculum expectations (by grade level and content area).
   - Relationships across grade levels and content areas (establishing articulation and coordination).
   - Learner objectives and their validation and measurement within the system.
   - Supportive material needed to deliver the curriculum.

- Instructional materials and references for specific objectives.
- Instructional strategies recommended for effective attainment of objectives.

4. Design and implement training for administrators in the measurement of learning and progress. Administrators need to know and be able to do the following:
   - Monitor achievement results as measured for students, classrooms, and schools.
   - Manage a range of assessment instruments used—all grade levels, all content areas.
   - Implement methods for disaggregating data for instructional and curriculum decision-making.

5. Structure · administrator training activities to build and assure skills in organizational intervention and on how to use data in determining courses of action. Components to include are as follows:
   - How school based plans and actions are best determined and what data is used to determine selections.
   - How to determine and take courses of action congruent with best practice.
   - How to design and conduct training and professional development focused on assessed needs.
   - How to provide resources to schools in accordance with curriculum objectives and needs.
   - How to intervene in the operations of a school, based on rational and appropriate evidence of need.

Feedback from teachers in dozens of curriculum audits indicates that many administrators often avoid personal involvement in curriculum management and instruction and fail to accept accountability for learning. However, if a school system is to be effective, successful, and proficient in meeting its goals, the administrator must be an instructional leader and an exemplary curriculum manager. Anything less in terms of role expectations will preclude organizational success in design and delivery of learning.

Strategy 45

Provide Differentiated Staff Development

*Staff development is differentiated for staff
and built around the CMSi staff development criteria.*

Strategy 45: WHAT

Everyone understands the need for staff development if you are going to get higher student achievement. We will only do this through the development of staff capacity. Unfortunately, little time has been invested in the staff to help them affect positive growth and change for the school or district. School improvement plans often budget money for things rather than growth. Then we wonder why change does not take place.

Many districts spend money on additional staff, more equipment, and new programs and still student achievement does not take place. When we examine these districts there is always a common thread—little or no staff development. And when there is staff development, the approach used usually violates the research on change. An all-day or half-day workshop is conducted and staff is told to "go forth and do." There is seldom a support system in place to fully institutionalize an intervention.

The Curriculum Management Improvement Model recommends following certain criteria when designing staff development endeavors. These criteria are listed in *Figure 22*.

Figure 22

Design Characteristics of Effective Staff Development
Curriculum Management Systems, Inc.

The School System's Staff Development Program:

1. Is based on policy that directs staff development activities and actions to be aligned to and an integral part of the district strategic and/or long-range plan and its implementation.
2. Fosters a norm of improvement and development of a learning community.
3. Provides for organizational, unit, and individual development in a systemic manner.
4. Is provided for all employees.
5. Expects each principal/supervisor to be a staff developer of those supervised.
6. Is based on a careful analysis of data and is data driven; uses disaggregated student achievement data to determine adult learning priorities; and monitors progress and helps sustain improvement of each person carrying out his/her work.
7. Focuses on research-based approaches that have proven to increase productivity.
8. Provides for the following: initiation, implementation, institutionalization and renewal.
9. Is based on adult human learning and development theory and directs staff development efforts congruent with system priorities as reflected in the district the plan.
10. Uses a variety of staff development approaches.
11. Provides the follow-up and on-the-job application necessary to ensure improvement.
12. Requires an evaluation process that includes multiple sources of information, focuses on all levels of the organization, and is based on actual changed behavior and increased student achievement.
13. Provides for system-wide management oversight of staff development efforts.
14. Is supported with the necessary funding and resources needed to deliver staff development called for in the district-wide strategic and/or long-range plan, and is reflected in the system's budget allocations.

One of the greatest violations, when staff development takes place, is the lack of recognition that people come to training with different experience, capabilities, and knowledge. It is essential that we provide differentiated training to move people toward the implementation of a new behavior.

Strategy 45: WHY

Just as we want teachers to differentiate their instruction in the classrooms so students are receiving learning opportunities at the right level of difficulty, so we must do this for our adult learners. In fact, adult learners are probably less tolerant than young people are when we are not at the right level of training. Educators are a very heterogeneous group of people, and training situations need to take this into consideration.

The most important reason for differentiation is that if we don't address it, we decrease the likelihood of moving our staff toward the change desired. We must understand variation in learners. Often, just giving people a choice of whether to attend increases attendance and attention to the learning. Certainly we can use the more experienced individuals in the setting to help mentor the others attending the sessions. Ideally we should have different professional development opportunities to meet the varying needs of our staff with respect to a new intervention in the system.

There is one caution here. We note frequently that teachers are given a potpourri of fragmented staff development offerings. District officers have often used this approach in an attempt to meet the differing needs of staff, but then in the process fail to focus on the changes mandated by the district's priorities. First, and foremost, the staff development efforts must be aligned to the district goals for change.

Strategy 45: HOW

We want to say, "Just do it," but a few steps are listed below that can help you implement this strategy.

1. Educate all individuals responsible for staff development training in effective adult learning approaches and address the need to differentiate the training.
2. Align all staff development activities to planned priority goals for change. These activities need to be included in the district and school improvement plans (see Strategies 40 and 41).
3. Create staff development plans using the CMSi criteria presented earlier in this strategy.
4. Evaluate the effectiveness of staff development activities in addressing the differing needs of the trainees and in changing their behavior.

Strategy 46

Link Resource Allocation to Goals, Objectives, Priorities, and Diagnosed Needs of the System

The district and school budgets are built after the planning and illustrate how moneys have been distributed to focus on the changes / goals of the district and school plan.

Strategy 46: WHAT

For years, school programs, services, and activities were created, planned, proposed, and terminated because of "insufficient funds." Budget processes preceded curriculum decisions, and curriculum initiatives had to be modified, reduced, or reconfigured to fit limited availability of funding. In a way, it was like "cutting the pattern to fit the cloth." Budget drove the curriculum, instead of the other way around *(English, 1987).*[16] The result was that educational quality was often compromised in the name of budget cutting, cost reduction, or retrenchment.

Something had to give. If educational leaders persisted at doing what had always been done, the result would never change. The result was not in accordance with what

---

[16] English, F. (1987). *Curriculum Management for Schools, Businesses, Etc. (get remainder of citation)*

communities and all but one state wanted *(Note 1)*.[17] Reform has been thrust on public schools, and the public is demanding three things from schools to gain economic confidence: alignment with resources available, prudence with funds provided, and demonstration of results and value for money spent. This relationship of demands is graphically represented in *Figure 23* shown below:

Figure 23

Components of Economic Confidence In Public Educational Institutions (Pomerantz Model)

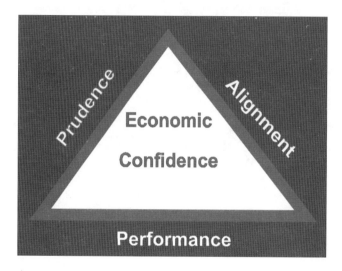

Prudence: Showing efficiency and setting financial house in order

Alignment: Living within means, adjusting budget to revenue levels

Performance: Tying priorities to results, showing gains in productivity

---

[17] Note: Every state in the United States, except Iowa, has prescribed a set of standards, exit competencies, or high stakes testing in the past 25 years in an attempt to reform public school education. Some states have even instituted "take overs."

School systems have not enjoyed substantial economic confidence in recent decades from the tax-paying public. Restraints on taxes for schools and demands for improvement in results have created a pattern of precious few discretionary dollars for schools to meet the increasing needs of clientele. To gain economic confidence, schools must live within the money provided by state and local governing authorities, show wise use of those funds (including demonstrations of benefit for given costs), and exemplify educational quality and acceptable results.

With schools under such intense financial scrutiny, some changes have been made in budgeting processes and operations. Schools have begun looking at what is expected of them and how well they are doing against those expectations, and they have proposed options and actions to address and deliver those expectations, and more. Schools have come up with different budgeting processes that are characterized by the following:

- Greater public and stakeholder participation in budgeting decisions, including teachers, principals, parents, students, and others.
- Better conceptualizations of what program alternatives will produce in measurable results. Gains in achievement have been attached to specific initiative requests for funding. Failure to produce the intended result may mean withdrawal of those funds in future budgeting. Performance has been promised, and it has been monitored.
- Program operations, measured results, and educational activities have been designed to connect to budget proposals, with clear definitions of cost and benefit. Options for delivery that may accomplish the objective at less cost have been included.
- Assessment feedback balanced against costs has been used to determine whether program options and operations are continued, terminated, or modified.

In school systems, budgeting is changing and it is placing curriculum and program planning ahead of budget allocations. Allocations then follow the priorities of the system until the resources are exhausted. These new approaches indicate greater gains in productivity if benefits can be increased and costs can be decreased.

Strategy 46: WHY

School leaders have a new set of demands facing them from the funding public–the schools must demonstrate what they want, why, and what will happen if they are funded. Not only that, but budget requests have to be made in programmatic increments and whole activities, instead of in line items and tabulations of costs. Unless school leadership can recover the economic confidence of the public, the future of public schools may continue to be in jeopardy.

There is another key reason for changing the methods of budgeting, other than for credibility. Curriculum-driven budgeting also produces greater cost-benefit relationships. When scrutinized by cost and return, program components change and improve to meet the higher standard of efficiency. More "bang for the buck" results as program managers find new, better, and less expensive ways to meet their mission. Moreover, once people see a tangible connection between an educational program increment (or alternative), the program component gains greater likelihood of funded support because of its clarity and definition of characteristics. Line-item proposals, which often read as "percentage" increases, do not provide that type of tangible connection between action, cost, and predicted result.

With diminishing financial resources to meet widening educational needs, school organizations can ill afford to keep trying to operate "business as usual." It is critical that purpose, options of delivery, and cost relationships be aggregated by program increments to demonstrate tangible connections between costs and benefits of educational activities.

Strategy 46: HOW

Try these ten steps to link resources to school organizational goals, planning, and results (school level):

1. Set up a program list that defines the major activities within the school. At least 15 to 20 programs need to be identified. Examples include: kindergarten, art, music, basic instruction (core academic areas), library services, technology services, custodial services, extra curricular activities, staff development, etc.).

2. Aggregate all costs incurred by these program areas for the previous year. Include all line items such as salaries, supplies, benefits, etc. Do not separate cost items unless they characterize a major activity of the school. The object is to change how people perceive the budget. It should be seen as a collection of program activities, not a long list of line-item costs.

3. Assign a manager or coordinator (administrator, employee, patron or non employee) to chair each program area planning team. Invite the community to be involved-bring them all in as much as possible.

4. Each program area planning team sets it own schedule, with meetings after 5 p.m. to facilitate parent participation. Each team is to develop a set of program increments for their program. Each increment will represent a portion of the program that may or may not be funded. (See Item 7 below).

5. Set a school-wide budget planning team meeting schedule. Includes two members from each program area planning team—one employee, one citizen (not employed by the system).

6. Provide reference materials and information to each member of the school-wide team, including budget history, budget areas by program, etc.

7. Set increment ranges for each program area budget. It is recommended that each program area budget develop one increment that costs less (2 to 5 percent) than the previous year, but only if at that level it would be able to function (presumably at a lower level of quality). Then include at least two more increments that if funded would add additional services or activities to the program.

8. Each program area planning team prepares its three or more increment packages. Packages are discrete parts of a greater program that has a base package and two or more add-on packages.

9. Program area teams then submit their list of program packages. They packages are assembled by the school and then rank-ordered in order of preference by the school-wide committee (use nominal group techniques). Once the program packages are all rank-ordered (some add-on packages may be a higher priority than the base package of another program) by the committee, it is possible to see

where the funds run out and which program packages the school will not be able to fund and will have to abandon.

10. Publish the priority-ranked list of budget requests from highest priority descending to lowest priority, and illustrate (with a drawn line) where the current funding level ends. Disseminate this list, with ranking and cost information, to the community, to the school superintendent, and to others interested in the quality of education within the school.

11. (Optional) Move toward connecting information about results and effects of program activities as a part of the budget planning activity. Programs that successfully demonstrate increases in productivity or achievement naturally would be more attractive for funding. Using the paucity of resources more intelligently would be the result.

This budget configuration will make it abundantly clear what the school activities are, what they cost, and how the school is unable to do everything it is asked to do without additional funding. For the first time, what's at stake will also be evident-not cost items (supplies, etc.), but program activities for the school's clientele. Very often, once the community sees that money falls short of delivering quality educational services desirable for a given school, additional resources are provided. Money isn't usually the problem–the will to spend it is often the problem. With the tangible connection clearly made between costs and program activities, better financial support is more likely than in the past.

Strategy 47
Provide Qualified and Adequate Personnel

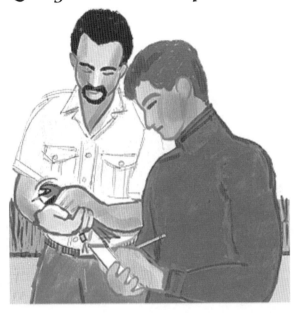

There are qualified and adequate school personnel in each position.

Strategy 47: WHAT

The process of education is complex and difficult. Successful education requires professionals trained in the many skills needed to effectively organize curriculum and deliver it to the students. If that were not the case, schools could be staffed with anyone off the street and the schools would produce learning. We know from experience that this is not the case, and to say that it is an insult and a great disservice to the many competent people working in schools today. We've found great disorganization of curriculum and poor teaching and classroom management in numerous school districts that employ noncertified teachers and inadequately trained administrators. Further, recent research demonstrates a strong correlation between student achievement and high-quality certification. This means that all school personnel who come in contact with students must be competent in their jobs in order for the school to be successful in producing the desired levels of learning.

Everyone who works in a successful school plays a vital role. Custodians keep the school facility clean and warm (see Strategy 50), teacher assistants contribute to the delivery of the curriculum, principals provide management and leadership services, and teachers provide the most important function–they teach. Competent people should occupy all positions. Unfortunately, competence is not always the rule, even though staff may possess proper certification.

Certification and competence are not synonymous. We observed the use of many unsuccessful instructional strategies over and over again. We observed schools where the academic learning time is very low–where students are not engaged in the lesson. We observed classrooms where no lesson was discernible. We observed schools where many teachers are not engaged with the students; instead, they are out of the classroom, working at their desks, or reading a newspaper, but they were not working with the students. What is significant is that these are not a few isolated cases, they are the majority in some schools.

Some authors have suggested that 5 to 20 percent of the teaching force is incompetent. We don't know if these figures are accurate, but we do know that even the most conservative estimate is too high and would produce disastrous results. For instance, the lowest estimate, 5 percent, would be enough teachers to staff every school in Rhode Island. That means that every student's education in Rhode Island would be wasted. That is unacceptable. Our observations of hundreds of principals indicate that the same percentage of the administrators may be incompetent. This, too, is unacceptable.

Fully qualified and high-performing teachers and administrators are required for each position in every school. Anything less is unacceptable, education is jeopardized, and students suffer.

Strategy 47: WHY

Successful organizations, whether business, education, or athletic, employ highly competent people. A school is no different. A competent principal is needed to ensure that the curriculum is well designed, that the taught curriculum matches the written and tested curriculum (see Strategies 1 and 29), that the environment is safe (see Strategies 49 and 50), that instruction is effective, and that teachers have the resources needed to run effective classrooms. When any of these is not done well, student learning is negatively affected.

It cannot be said enough: teachers provide the most important function–they teach. High-quality instruction is the cornerstone of any effective school, and it separates ineffective and marginal schools from effective schools. Without effective teaching, student learning is seriously at risk.

The bottom line is that all school personnel need to be competent and perform up to par before a school can be effective. The Board of Education, through its line administration, must ensure that all employees are qualified and performing adequately.

Strategy 47: HOW

Try these ideas for implementing this strategy:

1. Check your policies for personnel hiring requirements. Is the employment of only certified teachers and administrators required? If not, it must be addressed to the board. Does the policy require that only the most qualified candidates be hired for each position? Bold and successful districts announce that they want only the "best and the brightest" teachers and administrators. How does your district stack up?

2. Check your district's criteria for making hiring decisions. Do they include:

   For teachers
   - Observation of actual teaching?
   - Well-designed interviews?
   - Problem-solving exercises regarding instruction and classroom management?
   - Consideration of academic and professional preparation curriculums and academic records on both?
   - Compliance with state laws regarding employment and appropriate checks for criminal records?
   - Hiring of only the best and brightest teachers?

   These are some of the factors that must be considered. Some, like academic records, may seem strange. But they aren't, since there is a growing research base demonstrating that teachers' academic performance is strongly correlated to teaching quality and student achievement.

   For principals and principal supervisors
   - Thorough and well-designed interviews by representatives from all affected employee groups and senior administration?
   - Observation of a teaching sample, analysis of it, and reflective counseling with the teacher?

- Assessment of inter-rater reliability of the candidate's assessment of the teaching sample and predetermined ratings?
- Assessment of curriculum design and delivery philosophy and knowledge?
- Thorough interviews with previous employers?
- Compliance with state laws regarding employment and appropriate checks for criminal records?

No hiring system can ensure that only competent people are hired or that those who are competent will perform up to par. In cases where an employee is marginal or incompetent, other action is needed. This topic is addressed in Strategy 48.

Strategy 48

Remove Incompetent Staff

Marginal staff are coached to satisfactory performance or contracts are not renewed.

Strategy 48: WHAT

   As stated in Strategy 39, personnel appraisal systems should focus on professional growth for all school personnel. However, there are times when employees' skills or attitudes are less than what is required. In these cases, the district and school have a moral, ethical, and economic responsibility to provide honest and straightforward information to the employee regarding the deficiencies and specifically what resources it will make available to the employee for his/her use in improving his/her skill to fully competent levels. The resources should include training (specifically targeted to the areas of deficiency) and coaching by the principal and expert teachers. The coaching should initially be reflective in nature, but when improvement is not observed, the coaching needs to be much more direct to ensure that the employee understands his/her status and the role of the coaching and resource assistance.

   It is important to remember that it is the employee's responsibility to attain competency. The fact is that we cannot make other people improve, but we can provide resource assistance designed specifically to help them ameliorate their deficiencies. Once provided, use of the resources and improvement of skills are the work of the employee. This is why we continually advise districts not to say or write that they will help the employee improve or attain competency. Once this is said, the responsibility is off the employee and on the person making this statement. The promise implicit in the statement might never be fulfilled.

Strategy 48: WHY

Incompetence in any position in education cannot be tolerated. The employee evaluation process and other observations of work should detect incompetence. When it is determined that an employee is incompetent, it is the school board's (district level) responsibility to provide resource assistance that the employee may use to ameliorate the deficiencies. If after a predetermined time and provision of resource assistance the employee does not demonstrate adequate improvement, the employee should be dismissed from employment. Each state and many employee contracts provide processes for this action for each employee group, e.g., tenured and non-tenured teachers, administrators, and classified employees.

Some people will say that dismissal is cold and hard-hearted. We say it is the right thing to do. Schools were never intended as halfway houses or havens for incompetent principals, teachers, or custodians. Schools have always had the responsibility of educating young people, and they cannot do that well with incompetent personnel. School boards, through the line administrative structure, must ensure that the schools are staffed with only highly competent personnel. To do otherwise endangers student learning, the product of our schools, and further lowers our esteem in the eyes of the public.

Strategy 48: HOW

Use the following to assess your district or school in relation to Strategy 48.

1. Check your board policy and employee appraisal system manuals. Do they clearly state that each employee's contribution to the education process is highly valued and that the district actively works to hire and retain only highly competent employees in all position?
2. Check your personnel evaluation systems:
   - Are they based on research-driven criteria of quality performance? We recommend 20 to 40 hours of training each year.
   - Are they developed to distinguish between competence and incompetence?
   - Is the process focused on professional development (See Strategy 37.)?
3. Check your training programs for employee evaluators. Have evaluators been adequately trained to reach high inter-rater reliability levels? Specifically, do they:
   - Know what to look for in teaching and the in classroom?

- Adequately assess and analyze teaching?
- Reflect empirically-and research-supported instructional practices?
- Know how to and actually follow through when deficiencies are noted?
- Know coaching theory and demonstrate high quality coaching practices?
- Demonstrate competence in working with teachers (or other employees) to develop performance growth plans?
- Monitor professional growth plans?
- Demonstrate competence in operating in accordance with state, board policy and employee-contract-imposed due process?
4. Check your professional growth plan requirements and practices:
    - Are they designed to bring about improved classroom instruction?
    - Do they require that the plan be based on observed findings?
    - Do they require monitoring by the supervisor?
    - Do they allow for reasonable resource assistance from the district?

We suggest that you analyze the answers to these questions and take action as needed.

Another test to determine if your district is accurately evaluating employee performance is to select a 10 percent random sample of results of your evaluations for all employee groups for the past three years. What percentage was rated in each possible category for each employee group? We found that more than 99 percent of all teachers and administrators in a random sample from thousands were assigned ratings ranging from adequate to excellent. This is great news! What could be better? If this were the case, public education would be thriving and student achievement would be forever increasing. Unfortunately, based on what we have observed in thousands of schools and classrooms, particularly in poor inner-city schools, we doubt that the percentage is accurate.

What percentage of employees is assigned each rating in your school? If the large majority is assigned adequate or higher, your ratings are suspect and the evaluators may be denying employees valuable feedback about their performance level.

The second step of the test is to analyze professional growth plans. Take a small random sample. Do you find that the growth plans target the employees' primary functions? In our analysis of hundreds of teachers' professional growth plans, we found that the majority of them contained no targets or activities for growth of any kind, let alone targets which pertained to their primary function, teaching. Supervisors have an obligatory responsibility to ensure that all employees have growth plans.

Strategy 49

Provide a Quality Learning Environment

*There is a safe and productive learning
environment for all students.*

Strategy 49: WHAT

A safe and productive learning environment is a hallmark of effective schools. A safe environment is characterized as one in which students attend school without fear of harm from internal or external forces. Students know that they are expected to learn and achieve high expectations, but they do not have to fear punishment should they stumble. They know that their school is a safe place for learning and exploration.

Learning is targeted as the number one goal in a productive learning environment. It is announced on classroom bulletin boards, policies, and newsletters. All 50 strategies listed in this book contribute to a productive learning environment the written curriculum is high quality; the written, taught, and tested curriculums are aligned; instruction is high quality and academic learning time is high; teachers are actively involved with students and; administrators are frequently in classrooms and ensure that teachers have the proper tools and resources for maintaining high quality education in their classrooms.

All of these are needed to ensure a highly productive classroom learning environment.

Strategy 49: WHY

A safe learning environment is needed to free teachers and students from fears of harm and thereby allow them to focus on teaching and learning. As stated in Strategy 46, education is a complex process and learning is no less so. Of course it is possible to learn in the presence of harm, we have all heard of such cases, but our students deserve to learn in safe environments where learning is unfettered by such concern.

Strategy 49: HOW

We suggest the following for assessing and improving the safety aspect of schools:

1. First, is a safe learning environment a district and school priority? If it is not stated as such in policy and regulations and announced publicly, appropriate action needs to be taken.
2. Assess the staff. Do all understand that students deserve an environment that is safe from unreasonable punishment and ensure the same?
3. Are students free from of threats of abuse from other students or adults on or off campus? Is there a policy regarding this and is it followed?
4. Are appropriate measures in place to prevent people who do not belong in the school or on the school grounds from being present?
5. Are all staff aware of and do they follow requirements for reporting possible student abuse to Child Protective Service personnel?
6. Is an effective and efficient communication and cooperation system in place with the local police and other authorities?

To further create a productive learning environment, see the 'how' sections of the other 49 strategies in this book.

Strategy 50

Provide Quality Facilities

*Facilities are adequate and promote creative
and innovative approaches to learning.*

Strategy 50: WHAT

School facilities play a major role in the effective delivery of curriculum. They provide the home for teachers to create nurturing, productive, and creative learning environments and where students can explore education and learn to the best of their abilities.

Facilities that allow for this are physically safe and clean; classrooms are adequate in number to accommodate proper class sizes; the atmospheric climate is properly controlled; lighting is adequate; all mechanisms for handicapped people are in place, e.g., wheelchair ramps, automatic door openers, etc.; trash receptacles are plentiful; and toilet areas are clean and exist in proper numbers for both sexes.

Because the total number of students in most school districts fluctuates, enrollment projections are needed to inform long-range planning for facility construction, expansion, and consolidation. Long-range planning allows the district to ensure high-quality and cost-effective learning facilities for the students.

Strategy 50: WHY

The why of Strategy 50 is not cognitively new to any of us. Just as the maintenance of a proper and clean environment in our homes is important to the health and well-being of our families, the same is true for our schools. The school is a home away from home for students and it is also the place of their formal education. We have observed astounding differences in student attitudes toward education when schools are clean and inviting and when they are not. Students and teachers in clean, healthy, and safe schools tend to be more enthusiastic, happier, robust, and better focused on learning than in schools where the schools are unkempt and danger is present.

For example, we have visited schools in our curriculum management audits where classes were conducted in hallways full of noise and visual distractions, where the sidewalks were so cluttered that is was nearly impossible to move about without walking on trash and spilled food or hitting a bottle, where the bathrooms were so filthy that the students refused to enter them (and certainly we were repulsed upon doing so), and where the "Girls" and "Boys" signs on restroom doors were missing. Principals, teachers, and students in these schools described the impact; they said that they simply did not want to be there. We saw first hand what it was like to be required to stay in a place where there is no safe and clean provision for conduct of daily bodily functions, where dirt and filth are ever-present, and worse yet, a place where no one seems to care. One winter we visited a New England high school that had broken classroom windows. The temperature was very cold, to say the least. In all of these examples, the impact on learning was profoundly negative.

Strategy 50: HOW

Try these ideas for diagnosing your school environment as a place for creative and innovative teaching and learning. Tour your school with a teacher, a parent, and a student. Ask all to complete this brief checklist:

1. *Classrooms:* There are enough classrooms to accommodate proper class sizes and grade configurations.
2. *Trash receptacles:* There is one at the end of each hallway, in each classroom, and in every other room in the school. If we want people to dispose of their trash properly, they must have a proper place to put it.
3. *Toilet facilities:* They exist in proper numbers in each area of the campus and in the proper ratios for each sex.
4. *Toilet areas:* They are clean and hand towels and soap are present.

5. *Heating and ventilation:* The proper temperature is maintained in all classrooms.
6. *General cleanliness:* The classroom and other rooms are swept clean each day. Chalk and white boards are cleaned each day. Supplies and equipment are properly stored.
7. *Lighting:* Lighting is adequate for reading and the conduct of normal classroom activities.
8. *Theatre/gymnasium areas:* They adequate in size for use by all students and adequately furnished to accommodate all necessary school functions.

Based on your findings, develop and implement a plan for correcting deficiencies. Check with your central office, if necessary, to determine if enrollment projections are being completed and if plans are in place to ensure proper accommodation of students as enrollment fluctuates.

✃ *Analysis of Standard Six* ✃

Now it is time for you to evaluate the status of your school or school district on *Standard Six: Institute Effective District and School Planning, Staff Development, Resource Allocation, and Provide a Quality Learning Environment*. For each strategy think about what the current status of your situation is, and the changes you feel are needed. Write your responses in the spaces provided.

STRATEGY	CURRENT STATUS	CHANGES NEEDED
40. Create a Singular, Focused Multiyear District Plan Incorporating Change Strategies for Higher Student Achievement	❏Adequate ❏Not adequate	
41. Align School Plans to the District Plan	❏Adequate ❏Not adequate	
42. Meet the CMSi Plan Design Criteria	❏Adequate ❏Not adequate	
43. Implement Aligned Teacher Training to Reach District and School Goals	❏Adequate ❏Not adequate	
44. Implement Administrative Training Aligned to Curriculum, its Assessment, and District Plan Priorities	❏Adequate ❏Not adequate	
45. Provide Differentiated Staff Development	❏Adequate ❏Not adequate	

❧ Analysis of Standard Six Continued❧

46. Link Resource Allocations to Goals, Objectives, Priorities, and Diagnosed Needs of the System	☐Adequate ☐Not adequate	
47. Provide Qualified and Adequate Personnel	☐Adequate ☐Not adequate	
48. Remove Incompetent Staff	☐Adequate ☐Not adequate	
49. Provide a Quality Learning Environment	☐Adequate ☐Not adequate	
50. Provide Quality Facilities	☐Adequate ☐Not adequate	

❧ Summary

It is important to realize that no one strategy is going to make a difference to your schools, rather only the integration of the standards and the strategies over time will bring progress. This is illustrated as follows:

Six Standards and the 50 Characteristics

We encourage you to assess your system, whether as a district or a school, on the ideas presented in this publication. You can conduct a gap analysis as to where you are and where you could be regarding the 50 strategies. Directly following this page is a comprehensive list of all six standards and their components.

We believe it is surely time for all schools to be high-performing institutions, no matter whose measures are used. Once this occurs we can extend our curriculum further to include even more meaningful learnings so that students will not only function but thrive in the twenty-first century.

❧ *Fifty Characteristics*

Standard One

Establish a Well-Crafted, Focused, Valid, and Clear Curriculum to Direct Teaching

1. **Ensure External Assessment Target Objectives Are Embedded in the Written Content Standards and Are Linked to State Standards/Expectations**: There is a written set of district curriculum content standards that embed all external assessments administered to students and that are linked to state standards/expectations for every grade/instructional level and course offered.

2. **Have Clear and Precise District Curriculum Objectives—Content, Context, and Cognitive Level**: The district curriculum objectives, aligned to external assessment objectives, provide *clearly specified* content (skills, knowledge, concepts, processes, attitudes, etc.) to be learned; the context in which the learning must be demonstrated, including the test format; the appropriate cognitive level to be mastered; and the standard of performance-the degree of mastery required.

3. **Deeply Align Objectives from External Assessments**: Objectives based on external assessments are placed (embedded) in the curriculum in a "deeply aligned" manner (content, context, and cognitive level).

4. **Sequence Objectives for Mastery Well Before They Are Tested**: Objectives are placed in the sequence of learning at least six months to a year before the student must first demonstrate mastery on the external test.

5. **Provide a Feasible Number of Objectives to Be Taught**: There is a feasible number of objectives to be learned so that students can master them. A time range for each is noted. District time allocations for all subject areas/courses are in place from which to compare feasibility.

6. **Identify Specific Objectives as Benchmark Standards**: Some of the objectives have been identified as district benchmark standards to be used for feedback for learning progress, program value, curriculum redesign, promotion, etc.

7.	**Place Objectives in a Teaching Sequence**: The objectives are developed in a teaching sequence rather than in the order of state standard/framework strands and are presented to teachers in this same manner.
8.	**Provide Access to Written Curriculum Documents and Direct the Objectives to Be Taught**: The school-based administrators and teachers have in their possession current curriculum and instructional documents (e.g. scopes and sequences, course of studies, guides) for all curricular areas. Policy directs teachers to teach to the objectives and administrators to monitor their implementation.
9.	**Conduct Staff Development in Curriculum and Its Delivery**: School-based staff members receive quality training on the curriculum scope and sequence and the use of curriculum documents.

Standard Two

Provide Assessments Aligned to the Curriculum

10.	**Develop Aligned District Pre/Post Criterion-Referenced Assessments**: For each objective there are aligned, criterion-referenced assessment items-aligned for both content and context. From these items the district has secure district level, pre/post assessments aligned to each district objective and external assessments. Practice assessments are also available. All assessment items for each objective are equivalent/parallel. These tests will be given to students at the appropriate instructional level.
11.	**Have a Pool of Unsecured Test Items Objective**: The district provides multiple equivalent (unsecured) criterion-referenced assessments for each objective. These are provided to teachers for use in diagnosing prerequisite skills, acquisition, and mastery of the objectives.
12.	**Establish Secured Performance Benchmark Assessments**: The district has secured performance benchmark tests that assess some of the objectives for each grade level/course. These are administered as pre/post tests at the beginning and near the end of the school year.
13.	**Conduct Assessment Training**: The district provides adequate training in classroom use of aligned assessments for directing classroom teaching.
14.	**Use Assessments Diagnostically**: Teachers use the assessments to gain diagnostic data of student learning on the objectives (prerequisite skills acquisition and mastery) for program assessment and to direct instruction.
15.	**Teach Students to Be "Test Wise"**: Teachers teach students test-taking skills that are aligned to the type of high-stakes tests being administered at the national, state, and district levels.
16.	**Establish a Reasonable Testing Schedule and Environment**: The district staff and school staff provide a reasonable schedule of testing as well as a proper physical setting for all assessment situations.
17.	**Disaggregate Assessment Data**: District assessments, as well as external assessments, are disaggregated by student, teacher, course/class/grade level, gender, race, socioeconomic level, and primary language, and are used in making program and classroom decisions.
18.	**Maintain Student Progress Reports**: Teachers maintain individual student progress reports by district objectives; students and parents are knowledgeable about the student's progress on such objectives.

Standard Three **Align Program and Instructional Resources to the** **Curriculum and Provide Student Equality and Equity**	
19.	**Align Programs to the Curriculum to Ensure Congruity**: All formal and informal programs are investigated for their alignment to the district curriculum objectives, and modifications are made to ensure high alignment.
20.	**Use Research and Data that Document Results to Drive Program Selection, and Validate the Implementation of Programs with Action Research**: Programs selected for use are research and data driven. Further, the school staff members collect their own action research on the programs selected.
21.	**Evaluate Programs to Determine Effectiveness to Strengthen Student Achievement of Curriculum Objectives**: Programs are evaluated to determine effectiveness in achieving student achievement on the curricular objectives.
22.	**Ensure that Textbooks and Instructional Resources Are Aligned to the District Curriculum Objectives and Assessments in both Content and Context Dimensions**: The district has a process to ensure that textbooks and instructional resources are aligned to district objectives and assessments as well as other external assessments. Analysis includes deep alignment both at the content and context levels.
23.	**Use Technology in Design or Selection Procedures to Ensure Strong Connections to System Learning Expectations and Feedback**: Technology software is designed or selected based on strong alignment to the content, context, and cognitive level of the district objectives and assessments and its potential to enhance the quality of instruction and learning.
24.	**Provide Training in the Use of Instructional Resources and Their Alignment with System Curriculum Objectives-Content, Context, Cognitive Level**: Staff members have been provided quality training on the use of instructional resources in alignment with district objectives-focusing on the content, context, and cognitive level of the objectives (or external assessments).
25.	**Select or Modify Instructional Resources for Lessons to Ensure Full Alignment with System Objectives and Tested Learning**: Teachers select or modify instructional resources for lessons to ensure 100 percent alignment with the content and context of the district objectives and assessments including external assessments.
26.	**Place Students in Programs and Activities in an Equitable Manner and with Equal Access to the Curriculum**: Students are placed in programs/activities in an equitable matter with equal access to the curriculum.
27.	**Implement Effective Programs and Strategies with English Language Learners**: Effective programs and strategies for working with students whose primary language is not English are in place to focus on vocabulary development and reading comprehension approaches.

Standard Four
Use a Mastery Learning Approach
And Effective Teaching Strategies

28. **Implement a Mastery Learning Model**: School-based administrators and all instructional staff have been trained on the mastery-learning model and use it.

29. **Align Teaching to the Curriculum**: Teachers and other instructional staff align their teaching to the content, cognitive level, and in the context specified by the district objectives and/or other external assessments, especially if the district objectives do not have this type of precision.

30. **Provide Differentiated Instruction**: Teachers and other instructional staff modify their instruction based on ongoing diagnostic assessments, provide differentiated instruction based on student learning needs, and teach prerequisite knowledge as needed.

31. **Provide Practice to Master the Curriculum**: Teachers and other instructional staff teach to individual student mastery of the objectives, providing ample practice opportunities over time for both short- and long-term mastery.

32. **Use Effective Teaching Practices**: Teachers have high-engagement rates for all students and use a variety of effective teaching practices such as comparing, contrasting, classifying; using analogies and metaphors; summarizing and taking notes; reinforcing effort and giving praise; providing homework and practice; using nonlinguistic representations; using cooperative learning; setting goals and providing feedback; having students generate and test hypotheses; using cues, questions, and advance organizers; providing for active engagement of students; and giving the opportunity to respond to each question, metacognitive learning, etc.

33. **Provide Students With Differentiated Time to Learn**: Teachers and other instructional staff provide differentiated time for students to master the objectives, recognizing that students learn at different rates.

34. **Establish ILPs for Low-Achieving Students**: Individual Learning Plans (ILPs) are developed for students who are underachieving, as indicated by test data. Low quartile students and/or "bubble" students are provided intensive assistance to remediate deficiencies.

Standard Five

Establish Curriculum Expectations,
Monitoring, and Accountability

35. **State High Expectations for Achievement for Each Student**: The superintendent, senior officers, school-based administrators, and instructional staff articulate strong expectations for high student achievement for each student.

36. **Monitor the Curriculum**: Monitoring by district level officials, including the principal's supervisor, takes place regularly to determine the status of the school(s) and to coach the school-based administrators.

37. **Visit Classrooms and Provide Feedback**: Principal and/or other school-based administrators visit each classroom at least twice a week to monitor curriculum design and delivery alignment, quality of instruction, and classroom management, and to provide feedback to staff for affecting higher student achievement.

38.	**Use Disaggregated Data in the Decision-Making Process:** Principal ensures that all test data are appropriately disaggregated for teachers and used in decision-making.
39.	**Focus Staff Appraisal on Professional Growth:** The staff appraisal/evaluation process focuses on the professional growth of staff in the accomplishment of high student achievement.

Standard Six

Institute Effective District and School Planning, Staff Development, Resource Allocation, and Provide a Quality Learning Environment

40.	**Create and Implement a Singular focused, Multiyear District Plan Incorporating Change Strategies for Higher Student Achievement:** Planning is built into one comprehensive district improvement plan that consolidates all planning efforts. The plan focuses on two or three academic goals for multiyear periods of time. The plan incorporates effective change strategies, including professional development endeavors.
41.	**Align School Plans to the District Plan:** The school plan is aligned to a focused, district-wide plan for increased student achievement.
42.	**Meet the CMSi Plan Design Criteria:** The district and school plans meet the CMSI plan design criteria.
43.	**Implement Aligned Teacher Training to Reach District and School Goals:** Teachers receive and participate in ongoing training as part of reaching the goals in the district and school improvement plans.
44.	**Implement Administrative Training Aligned to the Curriculum, Its Assessment and District Plan Priorities:** Principal and other school-based administrators receive and participate in ongoing training directly related to curriculum design and delivery, curriculum monitoring, student and curriculum assessment and district and school improvement plan implementation.
45.	**Provide Differentiated Staff Development:** Staff development is differentiated for staff and built around the CMSi staff development criteria.
46.	**Link Resource Allocations to Goals, Objectives, Priorities and Diagnosed Needs of the System:** The district and school budgets are built after the planning and illustrate how moneys have been distributed to focus on the changes/goals of the district and school plans.
47.	**Provide Qualified and Adequate Personnel:** There are qualified and adequate school personnel in each position.
48.	**Remove Incompetent Staff:** Marginal staff are coached to satisfactory performance or contracts are not renewed.
49.	**Provide a Quality Learning Environment:** There is a safe and productive learning environment for all students.
50.	**Provide Quality Facilities:** Facilities are adequate and promote creative and innovative approaches to learning.

References

Andrews, R., Soder, R., & Jacoby, D. (1986). Principals' roles, other in-school variables, and academic achievement by ethnicity and SES. Paper presented at the annual meeting of the American Educational Research Association, San Francisco, April 1986.

Andrews, R., Soder, R. (1987). Principals instructional leadership and school achievement. Instructional Leadership, 44, 9-11.

Apple, M. (1979). *Ideology and curriculum.* London: Routledge and Kegan Paul.

Ashton, P., and Webb, R. (1986) Making a difference: Teachers sense of efficacy and student achievement. White Plains, NY: Longman Press, Inc.

Black and William, *Inside the Black Box: Raising standards through classroom assessment., Phi Delta Kappan.* http://www.pdkintl.org/kappan/kblac9810.htm

Blaze, J. (1987). Dimensions of effective school leadership: The teacher's perspective. American Educational Research Journal, 24 (4), 589-610.

Blaze, J. (1991). Journal of Educational Administration, 29(1), 6-21.

Bernstein, B. (1990). *The structuring of pedagogic discourse: Class, codes and control.* London: Routledge.

Berrien, F. (1968). *General and social systems.* New Brunswick, New Jersey: Rutgers University Press.

Bertalanffy, L. (1968). *General system theory: Foundations, development, applications.* New York: George Braziller.

Blau, P. and Scott, W. (1962). *Formal organizations.* San Francisco, CA: Chandler.

Bloom, B., Engelhardt, M., Furst, E., Hill, W., and Krathwohl, D. (1956). *The taxonomy of educational objectives: Handbook 1: Cognitive Domain.* New York: David McKay.

Chester & Beaudin. (1996). Efficacy Beliefs of Newly Hired Teachers in Urban Schools. Presented at the 1996 Convention of the American Education Research Association. Spring 1996, Vol. 33, No. 1, 233-257.

Cizak, G., Webb, L. and Kalohn, J. (1995, March). The use of cognitive taxonomies in licensure and certification test development: Reasonable or customary? Evaluation and the Health Professions, 18, 1, pp. 77-91.

Cole, M. (1977). Culture, cognition, and IQ testing. In P. Houts (ed.) *The myth of measurability.* New York: Hart, 116-123.

Danielson, D.(1986).*Teaching for Master.* Outcomes Associates, Monroe, Washington.

Davis and Sorrell. (1995) *Mastery learning in public schools.* http://chiron.valdosta.edu/whuitt/files/mastylear.html

Downey, C. (Fall 2001). Are your expectations clear regarding an instructional model. *Thrust for Educational Leadership,* Association of California School Administrator, Burlingame, California.

English, F. (2002, May). On the intractability of the achievement gap in urban schools and the discursive practice of continuing racial discrimination. *Education and Urban Society*, 34 (3), 298-311.

English, F. (2001). Theoretical cross-currents within the curriculum management audit: A preliminary and critically reflective probe regarding the issue of social justice and other perspectives within CMA standards. Unpublished paper. Advanced Curriculum Management Audit Seminar, Big Sky, Montana. 18pp.

English, F. and Steffy, B. (2001. *Deep curriculum alignment: Creating a level playingn field for all children on high stakes tests of accountability.* Lanham, MD. Scarecrow Educational Press. Inc.

English, F. (2002, May). On the intractability of the achievement gap in urban schools and the discursive practice of continuing racial discrimination. Education and Urban Society, 34, 3, pp. 298-311.

English, F. and Larson, R. (1996). *Curriculum management for educational and social service organizations* (2nd ed.). Springfield, Illinois: Charles C. Thomas.

English, F. (1993). *Deciding what to teach and test.* Newbury Park, CA: SAGE.

English, F. (1980, April). Curriculum mapping. *Educational Leadership,* 37 (7), 558-559.

Firestone, W., Fitz, J., and Broadfoot, P. (1999, Winter). Power, learning, and legitimization: Assessment implementation across levels in the United States and the United Kingdom. *American Education Research Journal,* 36 (4), 739-793.

Foundations For Success: Case Studies of How Urban School Systems Improve Achievement, September 2002, Washington D.C.: Council of Great City Schools

Frase, L. (1998). An Examination of Teachers' Flow Experiences, Efficacy and Instructional Leadership in Large Inner-City School Districts. Prepared for the 1998 Annual Meeting of the American Educational Research Association.

Frase, L. (2001). An Examination of the relationships among principal classroom visits, teacher flow experiences, and student cognitive engagement in three inner-city school districts.

Frase, L., English, F., and Poston, W. (2000). *The curriculum management audit: improving school quality.* Scarecrow Press. Maryland.

Gardner, H. (1983). *Frames of mind: The theory of multiple intelligences.* New York: Basic Books.

Gerth, H. and Mills, W. (eds and trans.) (1970). *From Max Weber: Essays in sociology.* New York: Oxford University Press.

Good. T. and Brophy. J. (2000*). Looking in classrooms.* Longman: New York

Gould, S. (1981). *The mismeasure of man.* New York: Norton.

Haladyna, T., Nolen, S., and Haas, N. (1991). Raising standardized achievement test scores and the origins of test score pollution. *Educational Researcher,* 20 (5), 2-7.

Hall, R. (1972). *Organizations: Structure and process.* Englewood Cliffs, New Jersey: Prentice Hall, Inc.

Hallinger, P., & Heck, R. (1996). Reassessing the principal's role in school effectiveness. Educational Administration Quarterly, 32(1), 5-44.

Heck, R. (1991). The effects of school context and principal leadership on school climate and school achievement. Paper submitted for presentation at the annual meeting of the American Educational Research Association,. San Francisco.

Heck, R. (1992). Principals instructional leadership and school performance: Implications for policy development. Educational evaluation and policy analysis, 14 (1):21-34, Spring 1992.

Heck, R., Larsen, T., & Marcoulides, G. (1990). Principal leadership and school achievement: Validation of a casual model. Paper presented at the annual meeting of the American Educational Research Association,. Boston.

Higgins, N. and Sullivan, H. (1981). *Teaching for competence*. Tempe, Arizona

Jencks, C. and Phillips, M. (eds.) (1998). *The black-white test score gap*. Washington, D.C. Brookings.

Kahne, J. and Bailey, K. (1999, Fall). The role of social capital on youth development: The case of 'I have a dream' programs. *Educational Evaluation and Policy Analysis* 21 (3), 321-343.

Kulik, J. and Kulik, C. (1987). Effects of ability grouping on student achievement. Equity and Excellence 223, 1-2, pp. 22-30.

Lehman, N. (1999) *The big test*. New York: Farrar, Straus & Giroux.

Likert, R. (1961). *New patterns of management*. New York: McGraw-Hill.

Linn, R. (2000, March). Assessments and accountability. *Educational Researcher,* 29 (2), 4-16.

Lewin and Shoemaker (1991) *Great [performances: Creating classroom-based assessment tasks*, Association for Supervision and Curriculum Development, Alexandria Virginia

Louis, K., & Miles, M. (1991). Managing reform: Lessons from urban high schools. School Effectiveness and School Management, 2(2), 75-96.

Madaus, G. and Kellaghan, T. (1992). Curriculum evaluation and assessment. In P. Jackson (ed.) *Handbook of research on curriculum.* (pp. 119-156). New York: Maxwell Macmillan International.

March, J. and Simon, H. (1958). *Organizations*. New York: John Wiley and Sons.

Marzono, R. (2001*). Classroom Instruction that Works*. http://www.mcrel.org

Marzano, R. (2001). How and why standards can improve student achievement. *Educational Leadership, 59,* 14-19.

Marzano R. (2000). *Transforming classroom grading,* Association for Supervision and Curriculum Development, Alexandria, Virginia

McDonald. *Testing and test anxiety.* http://www.inspiringteachers.com/articles/anxiety/

McLaren, P. (1994). *Life in schools: An introduction to critical pedagogy in the foundation of education.* New York: Longman.

McLaren, P. (1986). *Schooling as a ritual performance.* London: Routledge and Kegan Paul.

McTighe. (1999). *A framework for communicating student learning.* http://www.aac.ab.ca/class.html

Merton, R. (1968). *Social theory and social structure.* New York: The Free Press.

Mintzberg, H. (1983). *Structures in fives: Designing effective organizations.* Englewood Cliffs, New Jersey: Prentice Hall, Inc.

Miyaska, J. (2000). A framework for evaluating the validity of test preparation practices. Unpublished paper, American Education Research Association, New Orleans, Louisiana.

Moss-Mitchell, F. (1998). The effects of curriculum alignment on the mathematics achievement of third-grade students as measured by the Iowa Test of Basic Skills: Implications for educational administrators. Unpublished doctoral dissertation. Clark University.

National Commission on Testing and Public Policy. (1990). *Reforming assessment: From gatekeepers to gateway to education.* Chestnut Hill, MA: Boston College.

Nasaw, D. (1979). *Schooled to order: A social history of public schooling in the United States.* New York: Oxford University Press.

Neil, M. (2000, Spring). State exams flunk test of quality. *The State Education Standard*, 1 (2), 31-5.

Nielson. *Aligning Assessment with Learning Goals* (Science). http://www.enc.org/topics/assessment...current.shtm?input=FOC-001580-index

Nisbett, R. (1998). Race, genetics, and IQ. In C. Jencks and M. Phillips (eds.) *The black-white test score gap*. Washington, D.C.: Brookings, 86-102.

Oakes, J. (1985). *Keeping track: How schools structure inequality*. New Haven, CT: Yale University Press.

Parsons, T. (1951). *The social system*. Glencoe, Illlinois: The Free Press.

Perrone, V. editor (1991) *Expanding student assessment,* Association for Supervision and Curriculum Development, Alexandria, Virginia

Phye, G. (1997). Classroom assessment: A multidimensional approach. In G. Phye(ed.) *Handbook of classroom assessment*. San Diego, CA: Academic, 33-51.

Piffer, J. (1982). *Organizations and organization theory*. Boston: Pitman.

Pogrow, S. (1999, November). Rejoinder: Consistent large gains and high levels of achievement are the best measures of program quality: Pogrow responds to Slavin. *Educational Researcher* 28 (8), 24-27.

Popham, J. (2000). Teaching to the test: High crime, misdemeanor, or just good instruction? Unpublished paper. American Education Research Association, New Orleans, Louisiana.

Popham, J. and Baker, E. *(1970) Systematic Instruction*. Prentice Hall. New Jersey.

Poston, W. (1992). *Making schools work: practical management of support operations.* Corwin Press. California.

Poston, W. (1994). *Making governance work: TQE for school boards.* Corwin Press. California.

Price-Baugh, R. (1997). Correlation of textbook alignment with student achievement scores. Unpublished doctoral dissertation. Baylor University.

Robinson, G. and Brandon, D. (1994). *NAEP test scores: Should they be used to compare and rank state educational quality?* Reston, VA: Education Research Service.

Sacks, P. (1997, March/April). Standardized testing: Meritocracy's crooked yardstick. *Change,* 25-28.

Sager, R. (1992). Three principals who make a difference. Educational Leadership, Vol., 40, No. 5.

Shapon-Shevin, M. (1994). *Playing favorites: Gifted education and the disruption of community.* Albany, NY: SUNY Press.

Slavin, R. (1990). Achievement effects of ability grouping in secondary schools: A best evidence synthesis. <u>Review of Educational Research</u> 60, <u>3</u>.

Spring, J. (1988). *Conflict of interests: The politics of American education.* New York: Longman.

Steffy, B. and English, F. (1997). *Curriculum and assessment for world-class schools.* P. Short (ed.). Lancaster, PA: Technomic.

Sternberg, R. (1992). *Metaphors of the mind: Conceptions of the nature of intelligence.* New York: Cambridge University Press.

Stiggins, R. (March 13, 2002). Assessment for learning: A vision for the future. Education Week,

Stiggins, R., (1997) *Student-Centered Classroom.* Prentice Hall, New Jersey

Teddlie, C., Kirby, P., & Stringfield, S. (1989). Effective versus ineffective schools: Observable differences in the classroom. American Journal of Education, 97, 221-236.

Thompson, J. (1967). *Organizations in action.* New York: McGraw-Hill.

Thompson, V. (1961). *Modern organization. A general theory.* New York: Alfred A. Knopf.

Thompson, C. and O'Quinn (2002, June). *Eliminating the black-white achievement gap.* Chapel Hill, NC: The North Carolina Education Research Council.

Thorndike, R. (1951). Community variables as predictors of intelligence and academic achievement. *Journal of Educational Psychology.* 42, 321-338.

Twelve steps teachers can take to prepare students for high-stakes tests. National Education Association http://www.nea.org/issues/high-stakes/12steps.html

Tyack, D. (1974). *The one best system: A history of American urban education.* Cambridge, MA: Harvard University Press.

Valentine, J., Clark, D., Nickerson, N., & Keefe, J. (1981). The middle school principal,. Reston, VA. National Association of Secondary School Principals.

Wang, J. (1998, Fall). Opportunity to learn: The impacts and policy implications. *Educational Evaluation and Policy Analysis.* 20 (3), 137-156.

Warren. *Mastery learning:* A basic introduction. http://allen.warren.net/ml.htm

Webb, N. (2002). An analysis of the alignment between mathematics standards and assessments for three states. Unpublished paper. American Education Research Association, New Orleans, Louisiana.

Webb, N. , Horton, M. and O'Neal, S. (2002). An analysis of the alignment between language arts standards and assessments in four states. Unpublished paper. American Education Research Association, New Orleans, Louisiana.

Wells, H. G. (1961). The outline of history. Garden City, NY: Doubleday.

Wenniger, E. (1975). Entropy, equilibrium, and organizations: Problems of conceptualization. In A. Melcher (ed.) *General systems and organization theory: Methodological aspects.* Kent, Ohio: Kent State University Press, 23-31.

Wiggins, G. (November, 1993) Assessment, authenticity, context and validity. *Phi Delta Kappan,* Blooming, Indiana

Wilkins, J. (2000, April). Characteristics of demographic structures and their relationship to school-level achievement: The case of Virginia's standards of learning. Unpublished paper. American Education Research Association, New Orleans, Louisiana.

Wimpleberg, R., Teddlie, C., & Stringfield, S. (1989). Sensitivity to context: The past and future of effective school research. Educational Administration Quarterly, 25(1), 82-107. Anderson, S., et al. (1975) *Encyclopedia of educational evaluation,* San Francisco: Jossey-Bass

Zellmer, M. (1997). Effect on reading test scores when teachers are provided information that relates local curriculum documents to the test. Unpublished doctoral dissertation, Marquette University.

About the Authors

Carolyn J. Downey is currently Associate Professor of Educational Leadership in the College of Education at San Diego State University. She formerly was the Superintendent for the Kyrene School District, Phoenix-Tempe, Arizona. Dr. Downey has written books and numerous articles. She is the author of the training program "Walk-Throughs and Reflective Feedback for Higher Student Achievement." She has conducted many audits and was the major architect of the External Evaluation Process for Low-Performing Schools in California. She received her M.S. from the University of Southern California and her Ph.D. from Arizona State University.

Fenwick W. English is currently Distinguished Professor of Educational Administration in the College of Education at the University of North Carolina, Chapel Hill, North Carolina. Dr. English is the originator of *curriculum mapping*, as well as the *curriculum management audit*. He has written twenty books and over one hundred journal articles as well as conducted forty curriculum audits in twenty years in the United States and abroad. He received his B.S. and M.S. from the University of Southern California and his Ph.D. from Arizona State University.

Larry E. Frase is the author or editor of eighty professional journal articles and twenty-three books, including *Top Ten Myths in Education: Fantasies American's Love to Believe*, *School Management by Wandering Around*, *Maximizing People Power in Schools*, and *Teacher Compensation and Motivation*. He is also co-author of *Walk-Throughs and Reflective Feedback for Higher Student Achievement*. Larry served as a teacher and assistant superintendent for six years in Arizona and New York, and as superintendent for eight years at the Catalina Foothills School District in Tucson, Arizona. He has served as lead auditor on thirty-two curriculum management audits and as auditor on twenty curriculum management audits.

Raymond G. (Jerry) Melton is currently the President of Mountain Bear, Inc., an educational management-consulting firm. He was formerly the Director of the Network for Educational Development for the greater St. Louis (Missouri) metropolitan area and prior to that Director of the National Academy for School Executives (NASE) for the American Association of School Administrators (AASA) in Arlington, Virginia. Dr. Melton created, along with Dr. Fenwick English, the National Curriculum Audit Center for AASA and was one of the original trainers of curriculum management auditors. He has conducted curriculum management audits and provided services and training widely across the United States as well as in other countries. Dr. Melton received his B.S. from Southwest Missouri

State University, his M.S. from the University of Missouri, and his Ed.D. from Arizona State University.

William K. Poston Jr. is a Professor of Educational Leadership and Policy Studies at Iowa State University in Ames, Iowa, and is the Executive Director of the Iowa School Business Management Academy. Dr. Poston is the originator of curriculum-driven budgeting, and he has led over sixty curriculum audits in the United States and other countries. He has written nine books and over forty journal articles, and he served as a superintendent for fifteen years in Tucson and Phoenix-Tempe in Arizona and in Billings, Montana. He is a past international president of Phi Delta Kappa. He received his Bachelor of Arts from the University of Northern Iowa and his Educational Specialist and Doctor of Education degrees from Arizona State University.

Betty E. Steffy is a retired professor of Educational Leadership and Policy Studies at Iowa State University. She formerly was a dean of a School of Education at a regional campus of Purdue University and served as Deputy Superintendent of Instruction in the Kentucky Department of Education. She served as a superintendent of schools in New Jersey and as a Director of Curriculum for a regional educational agency in Pennsylvania. She created the professional development model entitled *Life Cycle of the Career Teacher*. She is the author/coauthor of ten books in education and, numerous articles and symposium papers at UCEA and AERA. She earned her B.A., M.A.T., and Ed.D. from the University of Pittsburgh.

About Curriculum Management Systems, Inc.

Curriculum Management Systems, Inc. is a corporation whose mission is to become the premier international creator and producer of products and processes for education and training programs in curriculum design and delivery.

The company, located in Johnston, Iowa (a suburb of Des Moines) is working to transform concepts and ideas that improve achievement and enhance success of all students into effective and high quality products and to produce programs and services which facilitate efforts to enhance teaching and learning.

CMSi creates, markets, manages, and distributes a variety of programs and services for educational institutions. These products and services include the following:

- Development and quality control of curriculum management auditing services provided by contracted affiliate organizations.

- Creation and marketing of organizational improvement training services, including the following programs:
    - Maximizing student achievement through curriculum and assessment design and delivery (four day program)
    - Maximizing student achievement through system and support factors (four day program)
    - Leaving no child behind: 50 ways to close the achievement gap (two day program)
    - Coping with high stakes testing with the power of deep curriculum alignment (three day program)
    - Walk through supervision with reflective thinking to maximize student achievement (two day program)
    - Managing improvement with limited resources – performance-based budgeting (two day program)
    - Making governance work – board and administrative roles and responsibilities (one day program).

- Provision and delivery of diagnostic review and improvement recommendations for low performing schools in need of improving student achievement.

- Establishment of a wide range of customized curriculum support systems for local educational agencies to build in-house capacity.

To contact CMSi, please call (515) 727-1744 or write to CMSi, 6165 NW 86th Street, Suite 218, Johnston, IA 50131 USA. Email to cmsi@curriculumsystems.com.